Share your tried & true family favorites with us instantly at

www.gooseberrypatch.com

If you'd rather jot 'em down by hand, just mail this form to...

Gooseberry Patch • Cookbooks – Call for Recipes
PO Box 812 • Columbus, OH 43216-0812

If your recipe is selected for a book, you'll receive a FREE copy!

Please share only your original recipes or those that you have made your own over the years.

Recipe Name:

Number of Servings:

Any fond memories about this recipe? Special touches you like to add
or handy shortcuts?

Ingredients (include specific measurements):

Instructions (continue on back if needed):

Special Code: **cookbookspage**

Over ➤

Extra space for recipe if needed:

Tell us about yourself...

Your complete contact information is needed so that we can send you your FREE cookbook, if your recipe is published. Phone numbers and email addresses are kept private and will only be used if we have questions about your recipe.

Name:

Address:

City: State: Zip:

Email:

Daytime Phone:

Thank you! Vickie & Jo Ann

MODERN KITCHEN

· OLD-FASHIONED FLAVOR ·

Comfort foods your family loves,
using your favorite appliances

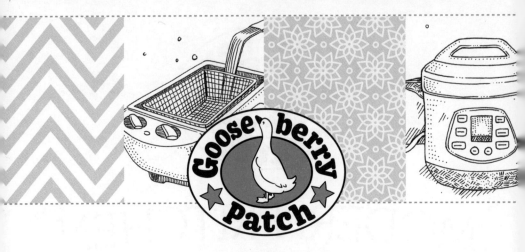

Gooseberry Patch

An imprint of Globe Pequot
246 Goose Lane
Guilford, CT 06437

www.gooseberrypatch.com

1•800•854•6673

Copyright 2018, Gooseberry Patch 978-1-62093-309-1

Do you have a tried & true recipe...

tip, craft or memory that you'd like to see featured in
a **Gooseberry Patch** cookbook? Visit our website at
www.gooseberrypatch.com and follow the
easy steps to submit your favorite family recipe.
Or send them to us at:

Gooseberry Patch
PO Box 812
Columbus, OH 43216-0812

Don't forget to include the number of servings your recipe makes,
plus your name, address, phone number and email address. If we
select your recipe, your name will appear right along with it...
and you'll receive a **FREE** copy of the book!

Contents

Dedication

To everyone who loves to share home-cooked meals with family & friends...no matter how busy you may be.

Appreciation

A hearty thanks to all of you who shared your most delicious recipes with us.

Meals in
An Instant

Cheesy Egg Casserole

Lynn Williams
Muncie, IN

This is a treat-yourself kind of weekend breakfast. If it's going to be a busy morning, prep the egg and sausage mixtures ahead of time; refrigerate separately. In the morning, just combine in the pot and go!

1 c. shredded Cheddar cheese
8 eggs, beaten
1/2 c. milk
1 t. salt, divided
1/2 t. pepper, divided
1 t. olive oil
1/2 lb. pork breakfast sausages

1 c. yellow onion, chopped
1 c. red pepper, chopped
2 T. fresh chives, minced
1 c. water
Garnish: sour cream

Wrap a 7" springform pan with aluminum foil, leaving some excess for handles on each side. Spray pan with non-stick vegetable spray; spread cheese in pan and set aside. In a bowl, whisk together eggs, milk, 1/2 teaspoon salt and 1/4 teaspoon pepper. Set aside. Add oil to a 5-quart electric pressure cooker; set on sauté. Add sausages; cook, stirring often, until browned. Add onion and red pepper; cook, stirring often, until tender. Stir in chives and remaining salt and pepper; transfer sausage mixture to pan. Place a rack or trivet inside pressure cooker; add water. Set pan on rack; pour egg mixture over sausage mixture. Close and lock lid; cook on high pressure for 12 minutes. Open pressure cooker using natural release method; let stand 10 minutes. Using the foil handles, remove pan from pressure cooker. Cut into wedges; serve with sour cream. Serves 6 to 8.

With an electric pressure cooker, you can make mealtime easy and fun! For the best results, before you start, be sure to check out the manual for yours, as the settings may vary from model to model.

Meals in an Instant
• ELECTRIC PRESSURE COOKER •

Steel-Cut Oatmeal & Fruit

Liz Blackstone
Racine, WI

*Oats cooked down into a sweet, creamy porridge your family
will love. This recipe makes plenty...leftovers can be covered
and refrigerated up to three days, then reheated in the microwave.*

3 c. water
3 c. milk
2 c. steel-cut oats, uncooked
2 T. butter
1/4 t. cinnamon

1/2 t. vanilla extract
1/2 to 3/4 c. dried cranberries,
   cherries or raisins
Optional: milk or cream

In a 5-quart electric pressure cooker, combine all ingredients except
optional milk or cream; stir gently. Close and lock the lid; bring up to
high pressure. Set heat to high. When cooker reaches high pressure,
reduce heat as low as possible while still maintaining high pressure.
Set timer and cook for 8 minutes. Open pressure cooker using natural
release method. Let stand for 15 minutes; if pressure is not completely
released, open valve. Serve hot, topped with milk or cream if desired.
Serves 4 to 6.

An old-fashioned cream pitcher of milk and a sugar bowl
filled with brown sugar add a sweet touch to a
simple breakfast of oatmeal.

Simple Brunch Quiche

Zoe Bennett
Columbia, SC

Make this quiche just the way you like it! Some delicious variations are Swiss cheese & crispy bacon or Monterey Jack with salsa and black olives.

1 c. shredded Cheddar cheese
6 eggs, beaten
1/2 c. milk
2 T. fresh chives, chopped

1/4 t. salt
1/8 t. pepper
1 c. water

Wrap a 7" springform pan with aluminum foil, leaving some excess for handles on each side. Spray pan with non-stick vegetable spray; spread cheese in pan and set aside. In a bowl, whisk together eggs, milk, chives and seasonings; pour over cheese in pan. Place a rack or trivet in a 5-quart electric pressure cooker; add water and set pan on rack. Close and lock lid. Select high pressure for 30 minutes, making sure the valve in the lid is closed. After 30 minutes, turn off pressure cooker and let stand 10 minutes. Open pressure cooker using quick release method. Remove pan using foil handles; let cool slightly and slice into wedges. Makes 4 servings.

Breakfast egg dishes like omelets, quiches and cheesy scrambled eggs are just as delicious at dinnertime. Fresh eggs can safely be kept refrigerated for 4 to 5 weeks, so go ahead and stock up when they're on sale.

Meals in an Instant
• ELECTRIC PRESSURE COOKER •

Cinnamon-Apple Pull-Apart Bread

Anna McMaster
Portland, OR

My kids just love pulling off pieces of ooey-gooey monkey bread. It's an easy treat that I'm happy to make for them.

1 c. water
3/4 c. sugar
1-1/2 t. cinnamon
2 12.4-oz. tubes refrigerated
    cinnamon rolls, quartered

3 Granny Smith apples, peeled,
    cored and diced
1/2 c. butter, melted

Add a rack or trivet to a 5-quart pressure cooker; add water. Wrap a 7" springform pan with aluminum foil, leaving excess for handles on each side. Grease pan; place on rack and set aside. Combine sugar and cinnamon in a cup; set aside along with icing packets from rolls. In a large bowl, toss together apples, roll pieces, cinnamon-sugar and melted butter. Spoon mixture into pan; set pan on rack. Close and lock the lid; cook on high pressure for 25 minutes. Open, using quick release method; allow to cool. Remove pan, using foil handles. Invert a plate over pan; flip to turn out rolls. Drizzle with reserved icing. Serves 6 to 8.

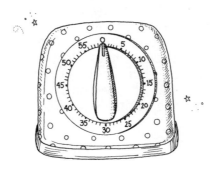

With an electric pressure cooker, allow at least 10 extra minutes to each recipe's time for the cooker to reach pressure and then to release pressure.

Caramel-Pecan Coffee Cake
Stephanie Eakins
Columbus, OH

Surprise your family with this luscious breakfast treat. A different-size pan may require a longer or shorter cooking time.

3 c. all-purpose flour
1-1/2 t. baking powder
1-1/2 t. baking soda
1/2 t. salt
3/4 c. butter, softened
1-1/2 c. sugar
3 eggs, beaten
1-1/2 c. sour cream
1 t. vanilla extract

1/2 t. almond extract
1/3 c. salted caramel baking
chips
3/4 c. brown sugar, packed
1 c. chopped pecans
1 t. cinnamon
1 t. nutmeg
Garnish: caramel topping,
vanilla icing

In a bowl, mix together flour, baking powder, baking soda and salt. In a separate large bowl, combine butter, sugar, eggs, sour cream and extracts. Beat with an electric mixer on low speed until smooth. Slowly beat in flour mixture until smooth. Gently fold in caramel chips; set aside. Spray a 6-cup Bundt pan with non-stick vegetable spray. In a small bowl, combine brown sugar, pecans and spices. Spoon 1/3 of brown sugar mixture into bottom of pan. Spoon in half of batter until pan is 1/3 full; spread evenly. Add another 1/3 of brown sugar mixture and remaining batter. (Pan should be no more than 3/4 full.) Cover top of pan with aluminum foil. Fold 2 long strips of foil and cross under pan to form handles. Add a rack or trivet to a 6-quart electric pressure cooker; add water. Set pan on rack. Close lid and steam valve. Set to manual, pressure, high, for 30 minutes. Open using natural release method. Using foil handles, carefully lift out pan to a wire rack; uncover and cool completely. Carefully flip over on to a plate. Drizzle with caramel topping and/or icing; sprinkle remaining brown sugar mixture on top. Serves 8 to 10.

Invite friends to chat over hot coffee
and a freshly baked coffee cake...
you'll be glad you did!

Honeyed Apple-Pear Sauce

Jill Burton
Gooseberry Patch

The best applesauce you ever tasted! Perfect after a family trip to the pick-your-own orchard.

6 Granny Smith apples, peeled, cored and cut into chunks
6 to 7 Bartlett pears, peeled, cored and cut into chunks

1 c. water
1/4 c. honey
3 T. butter

In a 6-quart electric pressure cooker, combine apples, pears and water. Close and lock the lid; set heat to high. When cooker reaches high pressure, reduce heat as low as possible while still maintaining high pressure. Set timer to cook for 2 minutes. Open using natural release method; let stand for 15 minutes. Stir in honey and butter. Using a potato masher or immersion blender, mash fruit to desired consistency. Cover and refrigerate up to 5 days. Makes 5 cups.

For perfect lunch-size portions, ladle homemade applesauce into pint-size canning jars.

Country Chicken Soup

Jill Valentine
Jackson, TN

Granny used to make the best chicken soup, simmering it for hours on the back of the stove. I think her secret was the love she added... but this soup is almost as good and so much quicker!

3-1/2 to 4-lb. chicken,
    fat trimmed
1 carrot, peeled and halved
1 onion, halved
1 stalk celery, halved
2 sprigs fresh parsley

1/2 bay leaf
1/4 t. pepper
6 to 6-1/2 c. water
salt to taste
1 c. cooked rice or orzo pasta

Discard giblets and neck from chicken. Place chicken in a 6-quart electric pressure cooker, breast-side up. Tuck vegetables and herbs around chicken. Add water to fill line in pressure cooker, just until chicken is covered. Close and lock lid; set heat to high. When cooker reaches high pressure, reduce heat as low as possible while maintaining high pressure. Set timer and cook for 30 minutes. Open using quick release method. Insert a sturdy wooden spoon in cavity of chicken; lift and tilt chicken so that broth runs back into pressure cooker. Remove chicken to a platter; let cool. Strain broth into a large bowl; through a colander lined with cheesecloth. Slice carrot and add to broth; season with salt. Chop chicken, discarding skin and bones; add desired amount of chicken to broth. Just before serving, stir in cooked rice or pasta. Makes 4 to 5 servings.

It is astonishing how short a time it takes
for very wonderful things to happen.
– Frances Hodgson Burnett

Meals in an Instant
• ELECTRIC PRESSURE COOKER •

Bacon-Veggie Soup

Courtney Stultz
Weir, KS

We always roast vegetables for our holiday meals, but sometimes I get a little carried away. So I took the extra cut-up vegetables and tossed them in my pressure cooker with some bacon to make soup. It is delicious! You could also use leftover turkey instead of bacon, or even make it meatless.

4 slices turkey or pork bacon,
    chopped
1 rutabaga, peeled and diced
1 turnip, peeled and diced
1 parsnip, peeled and diced
1 sweet potato, peeled and diced
8 Brussels sprouts, trimmed
    and cut in half

1 c. carrot, peeled and diced
1 c. fennel bulb, diced
1/2 c. leek or onion, chopped
1 t. dried parsley
1/2 t. Italian seasoning
1 t. salt
1/2 t. pepper
5 c. chicken or turkey broth

Combine all ingredients in a 6-quart electric pressure cooker; stir well. Close and lock lid; set to high and cook for 15 minutes. Open pressure cooker using natural release method for 10 minutes; manually release remaining pressure. Makes 8 servings.

Sautéed onion adds flavor to homemade soup. Simply sauté chopped onion in a little oil before adding the broth and other ingredients.

Eggplant & Okra Stew

Jennie Gist
Gooseberry Patch

*This hearty vegetable stew is delicious hot, at room temperature
or even chilled. Serve with crusty bread.*

2 eggplants, peeled and cut
   into 2-inch cubes
2 t. salt, divided
4 T. olive oil, divided
1 onion, chopped
4 cloves garlic, minced
28-oz. can peeled whole
   tomatoes, crushed

1/4 c. vegetable broth
1 green pepper, finely chopped
2 stalks celery, chopped
1/2 t. dried oregano
pepper to taste
1 lb. okra, ends trimmed and
   cut into 1-inch pieces
2 T. red wine vinegar

In a paper towel-lined colander, sprinkle eggplant cubes with one
teaspoon salt; let drain for 30 minutes. Rinse well and pat dry. Add
one tablespoon oil to a 5 to 6-quart electric pressure cooker; set on
sauté. Add onion and cook until softened, about 5 minutes. Add
remaining oil, garlic and eggplant. Cook, stirring occasionally, for about
5 minutes. Add tomatoes with juice, vegetable broth, green pepper,
celery, oregano and remaining salt and pepper. Lock the lid and set on
high. When cooker reaches high pressure, reduce heat as low as
possible, while maintaining high pressure. Set timer and cook for
3 minutes. Open using quick release method; stir. Eggplant and pepper
should be tender, but not mushy. If too much liquid remains, simmer,
uncovered, until partially reduced. Add okra; partially cover and cook
on medium heat for about 10 minutes (without pressure), until tender.
Drizzle with vinegar before serving. Serves 4.

Wide-rimmed soup plates are perfect for serving
saucy pasta dishes as well as hearty soups. Garnish
with a baguette slice set on the rim.

Creamy Tomato-Basil Parmesan Soup

Stephanie Eakins
Columbus, OH

This might be the best tomato soup you ever tasted! Wonderful alongside a grilled cheese sandwich, or just to sip from a mug on a chilly day.

2 14-1/2 oz. cans fire-roasted
    diced tomatoes
4 c. vegetable or chicken broth
1 c. celery, chopped
3/4 c. carrot, chopped
1/2 c. onion, chopped
1/4 c. fresh basil, chopped,
    or 1 T. dried basil

1 t. dried oregano
1/2 t. garlic powder
1 c. grated Parmesan cheese
1-1/2 c. half-and-half, warmed
1 t. salt
1/2 t. pepper

In a 5-quart electric pressure cooker, combine tomatoes with juice, broth, vegetables, basil and seasonings; stir. Close and lock lid; cook on manual high pressure for 25 minutes. Open pressure cooker using natural release method for 10 to 20 minutes. Using an immersion blender, blend vegetables until smooth. Add Parmesan cheese and half-and-half; blend again until well mixed. Season with salt and pepper. If desired, add a little more basil or oregano to taste. Makes 6 servings.

Lacy cheese crisps are delicious soup toppers. For each, sprinkle 2 tablespoons shredded Parmesan cheese onto a baking sheet lined with a silicone baking mat. Allow 4 inches for spreading. Bake at 400 degrees for 6 to 8 minutes, until golden. Cool slightly and add to soup bowls.

Southwestern Black Bean Chili

Athena Colegrove
Big Springs, TX

Serve bowls of this spicy meatless crowd-pleaser with a pan of warm corn muffins or a big stack of warm flour tortillas.

1 lb. dried black beans, rinsed
    and sorted
1/4 c. olive oil
2 onions, chopped
1 green or yellow pepper,
    chopped
1 red pepper, chopped
3 cloves garlic, finely chopped
2 c. water
1 T. chili powder

2 t. dried oregano
2 10-oz. cans diced tomatoes
    with green chiles
2 t. ground cumin
1 t. salt, or more to taste
1/8 t. cayenne pepper
Garnish: sour cream, shredded
    Cheddar cheese, sliced green
    onions

Place beans in a deep bowl; add enough water to cover by 2 inches. Soak for 8 hours or overnight. Drain; rinse and set aside. In a 5-quart electric pressure cooker, heat oil over medium-high heat. Add onions and cook for about 3 minutes. Add peppers and garlic; cook for about 2 minutes, until garlic is fragrant, about 2 minutes. Add beans, water, chili powder and oregano; stir. Close and lock lid. Set heat to high. When pressure cooker comes to high pressure, reduce heat as low as possible while still on high pressure. Set timer and cook for 10 minutes. Open pressure cooker using natural release method; let stand for 10 minutes. Beans should be tender, yet still slightly firm. Stir in tomatoes with juice and seasonings. Bring to a boil, uncovered, over medium-high heat. Cook, stirring occasionally, for 8 to 10 minutes, until liquid has cooked down slightly. Serve with desired toppings. Serves 4 to 6.

A bright-colored silicone muffin pan makes a terrific condiment server. Fill each cup with a different topping and let everyone help themselves.

Meals in an Instant
• ELECTRIC PRESSURE COOKER •

Linda's Taco Soup

Linda Peterson
Mason, MI

This is my very favorite soup, and it's ready to serve in a jiffy.

2 T. olive oil
1 lb. ground beef or turkey
1 c. onion, diced
2 T. taco seasoning mix
1 T. ranch salad dressing mix
14-1/2 oz. can stewed tomatoes
14-1/2 oz. can petite diced
   tomatoes
16-oz. can kidney beans, drained

16-oz. can pinto beans, drained
1 c. canned or frozen corn
4-oz. can diced chiles
2-1/4 oz. can sliced black olives,
   drained
8-oz. can tomato sauce
tortilla chips
Garnish: sour cream, sliced
   avocado

Press the sauté button on a 5-quart electric pressure cooker; add oil.
Brown beef and drain. Add onion and seasoning mixes. Continue to
cook until onion has softened. Add tomatoes with juice and remaining
ingredients except chips and garnish; stir together. Close and lock lid;
set to manual high pressure for 6 minutes. Open pressure cooker using
natural release method for 10 to 20 minutes; stir. Serve soup with
tortilla chips, topped with sour cream and avocado. Makes 6 servings.

Canned yellow or white hominy makes a tasty,
filling addition to any southwestern-style soup.

Old-Time Beef Stew

Jessica Eakins
Grove City, OH

This stew is so satisfying, enjoyed with some crusty bread. Sometimes I'll leave out the potatoes and serve this over mashed potatoes, or mashed cauliflower for a lower-carb meal.

2 T. oil
1/2 c. onion, diced
3 stalks celery, chopped
2 cloves garlic, minced
2 lbs. stew beef cubes
3 c. beef broth
1 T. tomato paste
1 t. Worcestershire sauce
1 t. sugar

1 t. dried thyme
1 t. salt
1/2 t. pepper
1/8 t. allspice or nutmeg
1 to 2 bay leaves
3 carrots, peeled and sliced
4 redskin potatoes, quartered
1/2 c. peas
Optional: 2 T. cornstarch

Heat oil in a 5-quart electric pressure cooker on sauté. Add onion and celery; cook for 3 to 4 minutes, until nearly tender. Add garlic; cook and stir for one minute, or until fragrant. Add remaining ingredients except cornstarch; stir well. Close and lock lid. Press the stew button to cook on high pressure for 35 minutes. Open pressure cooker using natural release method for 10 to 20 minutes; carefully remove lid. Discard bay leaves, if using. If a thicker consistency is desired, mix together 2 tablespoons of hot stew liquid with cornstarch; stir back into stew. Turn to sauté "less" mode; simmer for one to 2 minutes, until thickened. Makes 6 servings.

The sauté button is handy not only to sauté or sear...it can also be used to simmer and thicken sauces after cooking. Be sure to stir often, as the cooker will get quite hot.

18

Classic Chili

Nancy Wise
Little Rock, AR

*This thick, meaty chili is splendidly delicious...
wonderful for lunch or dinner.*

2 T. olive oil	1/2 t. dried oregano
1 onion, chopped	1 t. salt, or to taste
1 green pepper, chopped	1/8 t. pepper
2 lbs. ground beef	1/8 t. cayenne pepper
8-oz. can tomato sauce	1 to 2 16-oz. cans kidney beans,
1 c. beer or water	drained and rinsed
2 cloves garlic, finely chopped	saltine crackers
1 T. chili powder	Garnish: shredded Cheddar
1 t. ground cumin	cheese

Press the sauté button on a 5-quart electric pressure cooker; add oil, onion and green pepper. Cook until vegetables begin to soften. Add beef; cook until no longer pink. Stir in tomato sauce, beer or water, garlic and seasonings; stir and cook for about 2 minutes. Close and lock lid. Set heat to high. When cooker reaches high pressure, reduce heat as low as possible while still maintaining high pressure. Set timer and cook for 5 minutes. Open pressure cooker using natural release method; let stand for 10 minutes. Stir in beans. Simmer, uncovered, on medium heat for 8 to 10 minutes, until heated through. Serve with saltine crackers and shredded cheese. Makes 4 servings.

Stem and seed a green pepper in a flash! Hold the pepper upright on a cutting board. Use a sharp knife to slice each of the sides from the pepper. You'll then have 4 large seedless pieces ready for chopping.

Turkey-Vegetable Soup

Erin Brock
Charleston, WV

You don't need a turkey carcass to make fantastic turkey soup! Make sure the drumsticks fit in your pressure cooker...it's all right if the end of the bone touches the lid, as long as it doesn't block the vent. This soup is delicious with buttered warm dinner rolls.

2 T. olive oil
2 turkey drumsticks, skin
   removed
4 to 5 carrots, peeled and sliced
2 stalks celery, finely diced
1 onion, diced
6 c. chicken or turkey broth
1 c. sliced mushrooms

1/4 t. dried oregano
1/4 t. dried thyme
1 bay leaf
salt and pepper to taste
1 c. frozen petite peas, thawed
1 c. fresh or frozen green beans,
   chopped
3 to 4 T. fresh parsley, chopped

In a 6-quart electric pressure cooker, heat oil on sauté. Add drumsticks and brown on all sides, about 5 minutes. Transfer to a plate. Add carrots, celery and onion; cook for about 3 minutes, until beginning to soften. Return drumsticks to pressure cooker, meaty-side down; add broth, mushrooms and seasonings. Close and lock lid; set heat to high. When high pressure is reached, turn down heat as low as possible while still maintaining high pressure. Set timer and cook for 30 minutes. Open pressure cooker using quick release method. Transfer drumsticks to a plate; cool and shred meat. Discard bay leaf; skim off fat. Stir in shredded turkey, peas, beans and parsley. Simmer, uncovered, on medium heat for 5 to 8 minutes. Serves 6.

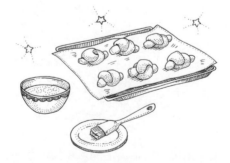

Freshly baked bread knots are cozy with hot soup. Tie refrigerated bread stick dough into loose knots, place on a baking sheet and brush with beaten egg. Bake as directed.

Everyday Vegetable Broth

Stephanie Mayer
Portsmouth, VA

I've found that good vegetable broth can be made with almost any mix of vegetables. There's no need to buy fresh veggies, either. I store veggie trimmings in a freezer bag until I have enough, then add the whole bag, frozen, to the pressure cooker and cover with water. No need to thaw. Use the broth in soups and recipes.

2 carrots, or 1 carrot and
   1 parsnip, peeled and cut
   into chunks
2 to 4 mushrooms, chopped
6 green onions, chopped
1 onion, quartered
4 stalks celery with leaves, cut
   into chunks

1 bulb garlic, halved
1 T. soy sauce
1/2 t. whole peppercorns
6 sprigs fresh parsley
2 sprigs fresh thyme
1 bay leaf
8 to 10 c. water
Optional: salt to taste

In a 6-quart electric pressure cooker, combine all ingredients except water and salt. Add enough water to cover vegetables by 2 inches. Close and lock lid; set heat to high. When high pressure is reached, turn down heat as low as possible while still maintaining high pressure. Set timer and cook for 7 minutes. Open pressure cooker using natural release method; let stand for 15 minutes. Remove lid. Strain stock through a large colander, lined with a double layer of cheesecloth and set over a large bowl. Press vegetables to extract all the liquid; discard vegetable pulp. If desired, season with salt. Cool completely. Pour into a covered container; refrigerate up to 4 days, or keep frozen up to 4 months. Makes about 1-1/2 quarts.

Save space in the freezer... ladle soup or broth into freezer bags, press out the air and lay flat. When frozen, the bags can be stacked.

Smoked Sausage & White Bean Soup

Sharon Tillman
Hampton, VA

I love to make this hearty soup on autumn weekends, after my friend Samantha and I come back from antiquing and seeing the fall colors. With a basket of warm, crusty bread, it's a meal in itself.

1 lb. dried navy beans, rinsed
   and sorted
1 to 2 T. olive oil
1 lb. smoked turkey sausage,
   sliced
1/2 onion, diced
2 cloves garlic, minced
3 carrots, peeled and chopped

2 stalks celery, chopped
1 t. fresh thyme, chopped
2 t. fresh rosemary, chopped
7 c. vegetable broth
3 c. fresh baby spinach
1 t. salt
1/4 t. pepper

Place beans in a deep bowl; add enough water to cover by 2 inches. Soak for 8 hours or overnight. Drain; rinse and set aside. Press the sauté button on a 5-quart electric pressure cooker. Add oil and cook sausage until browned; drain. Add onion; sauté until translucent. Add garlic; sauté for one minute. Turn sauté off. Add beans and remaining ingredients; stir. Close and lock lid. Select high pressure and set the timer for 20 minutes. Open pressure cooker using quick release method. To thicken the soup, use a wooden spoon to mash some of the beans against the side of the pot. Makes 6 servings.

When chopping onions, celery or green peppers, it takes only a moment to chop some extra. Tuck them away in the freezer for a quick start to dinner another day. No need to thaw before adding them to the pressure cooker!

Meals in an Instant
• ELECTRIC PRESSURE COOKER •

Chicken-in-a-Pot Stew

Emily Martin
Ontario, Canada

*We love this flavorful, easy-to-make dish. Remove the skin
from chicken thighs before cooking, if desired.*

6 carrots, peeled and cut
    into 1-1/2 inch chunks
2 onions, halved and
    thinly sliced
4 long strips lemon zest
4 sprigs fresh dill

4 chicken breasts
2 c. chicken broth
2 T. olive oil
salt to taste
2 T. fresh dill, chopped

In a 6-quart electric pressure cooker, combine carrots, onions, zest and
dill sprigs; add chicken, meaty-side down. Add broth; drizzle with oil
and season with salt. Close and lock lid; set heat to high. Set timer and
cook for 30 minutes. Open pressure cooker using quick release method;
stir in chopped dill. To serve, place each chicken breast in a large soup
bowl; top with vegetables and broth from pressure cooker. Makes
4 servings.

Want to try your favorite slow-cooker recipe in an electric
pressure cooker? If a meat dish cooks in 8 hours on low or
4 hours on high in the slow cooker, it will cook in 25 to
30 minutes in the pressure cooker. Choose the meat/stew
button for beef and pork...the poultry button for chicken
and turkey. Make sure the setting reads "sealing" and
not "venting" to ensure it's cooked properly.

Lentil & Sausage Soup

Shirley Howie
Foxboro, MA

I received an electric pressure cooker a few months ago, as an early birthday present, and am having so much fun experimenting with it and trying new recipes! This soup is one of the first things I made in it. It is very easy to make and tastes wonderful!

1 T. olive oil
1/4 c. onion, chopped
1 stalk celery, chopped
1 carrot, peeled and chopped
1/2 lb. chicken or pork sausage,
    casings removed
14-1/2 oz. can diced tomatoes
1 c. frozen spinach, thawed
    and drained

1 c. dried lentils, rinsed
    and sorted
4-oz. can sliced mushrooms,
    drained
4 c. beef broth
1 t. garlic, minced
1 t. salt
1/2 t. pepper

Set a 6-quart electric pressure cooker to sauté; add oil. Stir in onion, celery and carrot; sauté for 5 minutes. Add sausage and brown for about 5 minutes. Add tomatoes with juice and remaining ingredients; stir well. Close and lock lid. Set to manual, high pressure, and cook for 6 minutes. Open pressure cooker using natural release method, allowing about 20 to 25 minutes. Stir again and serve. Makes 4 to 5 servings.

Make lentil soup a fall favorite by using orange or red lentils...festive!

Split Pea Soup with Ham

Lynda Robson
Boston, MA

*This thick pea soup is quick & easy using a pressure cooker...
takes about 30 minutes from start to finish! For a little
different flavor, use smoked turkey instead of ham.*

1 lb. dried green split peas,
   rinsed and sorted
3 c. cooked ham, cubed
3 carrots, peeled and diced
3 stalks celery, diced
1 onion, diced
2 cloves garlic, minced

3 T. fresh parsley, chopped
1 bay leaf
4 c. water
1 t. salt
1/8 t. pepper
2 T. olive oil

In a 5-quart electric pressure cooker, combine dried peas, ham,
vegetables, garlic and herbs. Gradually add water; stir in salt and
pepper. Set heat to high and bring to a boil; do not stir. Drizzle with oil.
Close and lock lid. When high pressure is reached, reduce heat as low
as possible while still maintaining high pressure. Set timer and cook
for 6 minutes. Open pressure cooker using natural release method;
let stand for 20 minutes. Season with additional salt and pepper,
as needed. Makes 4 servings.

Dried peas and beans are nutritious, inexpensive and
come in lots of varieties...perfect for delicious family meals.
Before cooking, place beans in a colander, rinse well and
pick through, discarding any small twigs or bits of debris.

Spareribs with Smoky Tomato BBQ Sauce

Jason Keller
Carrollton, GA

No need to precook the ribs in boiling water...your pressure cooker does the job for you! Just add coleslaw and a pot of baked beans for a fantastic picnic meal.

3-lb. rack pork spareribs, cut
    into serving-size portions
salt and pepper to taste

1 T. olive oil
1 onion, thickly sliced
1 c. water

Prepare Smoky Tomato BBQ Sauce ahead of time; chill. Season ribs with salt and pepper; set aside. In a 6-quart electric pressure cooker, heat oil on medium-high heat until very hot. Working in batches, add ribs in a single layer; cook until browned on both sides, 5 to 7 minutes per batch. Transfer browned ribs to a plate. Add onion to drippings in pot and cook until soft, about 3 minutes. Return ribs to pot; add any juices from plate. Add water and sauce; bring to a simmer. Close and lock lid. When high pressure is reached, reduce heat as low as possible while still maintaining high pressure. Set timer and cook for 15 minutes. Open pressure cooker using natural release method; let stand for 15 minutes. Ribs should be falling-apart tender. Transfer ribs to a serving platter; skim fat from sauce and spoon over ribs. Serves 4 to 6.

Smoky Tomato BBQ Sauce:

1 c. catsup
1/4 c. apricot preserves
1/4 c. cider vinegar
3 T. tomato paste
2 T. red wine or water
2 T. olive oil

2 T. soy sauce
1 T. dry mustard
1 T. onion powder
2 t. smoked paprika
1 clove garlic, pressed

Combine all ingredients in a small bowl; whisk until smooth. Cover and refrigerate.

Brown Sugar Baked Beans

June Sabatinos
Salt Lake City, UT

Using a pressure cooker is a quick way to make a delicious scratch version of this holiday potluck classic. There are never any leftovers!

1 lb. dried navy beans, rinsed
    and sorted
10 c. water, divided
1 T. plus 2 t. salt, divided
8 slices thick-cut bacon, cut into
    1/2-inch pieces

1 yellow onion, diced
1/2 c. molasses
1 c. tomato purée
1/2 c. brown sugar, packed
2 t. dry mustard
1 t. pepper

In a large bowl, combine beans, 8 cups water and one tablespoon salt. Soak for 8 hours or overnight. Drain and rinse beans; set aside. Set a 6-quart electric pressure cooker on sauté and add bacon. Cook until crisp, about 5 minutes. Using a slotted spoon, remove bacon and transfer to a paper towel-lined plate. Add onion to bacon drippings; cook until tender, about 3 minutes. Add remaining water and salt, molasses, tomato purée, brown sugar, dry mustard and pepper; stir to combine. Stir in beans. Close and lock lid. Select high pressure and cook for 20 minutes. Open using natural release method. Check to make sure beans are tender; if not, continue to pressure cook, 5 minutes at a time. Select sauté and simmer, uncovered, for about 10 minutes, until sauce is reduced and thickened. Season with more salt and pepper, if desired. Makes 6 to 8 servings.

Light or dark brown sugar, which should you choose?
Light brown sugar offers mild sweetness, while dark brown
sugar adds richness. Try it in baked beans, where its
distinct molasses taste is especially delicious.

Pork Chops with Apples & Thyme

Cindy Neel
Gooseberry Patch

This dish is so easy to prepare, and the pork chops stay delightfully juicy. Serve with baked sweet potatoes for a delicious meal.

4 8-oz. bone-in pork loin or rib
  chops, 3/4-inch thick
salt and pepper to taste
1 T. olive oil
1 Fuji apple, quartered, cored and
  diced

2 shallots, chopped
1/2 c. chicken broth
1/2 c. hard cider or apple juice
1 t. fresh thyme, chopped
1 T. Dijon mustard
1 T. grainy brown mustard

Lightly season pork chops with salt and pepper; set aside. Add oil to a 6-quart electric pressure cooker; heat on medium-high heat until very hot. Working in batches, brown pork chops on both sides; transfer to a plate. Add apple and shallots to drippings; cook and stir for one minute. Add broth, cider or juice and thyme; bring to a boil, scraping up any browned bits from the bottom. Return pork chops and any juices from plate to pressure cooker, overlapping to fit. Close and lock lid. When high pressure is reached, reduce heat as low as possible while still maintaining high pressure. Set timer and cook for 7 minutes. Open pressure cooker using quick release method. Transfer pork chops to a platter; cover to keep warm. Allow liquid in pressure cooker to boil for a few seconds; stir in mustards. Serve pork chops topped with sauce from pressure cooker. Serves 4.

When using quick release on an electric pressure cooker, the steam will be very hot! Be sure to wear an oven mitt to protect your hand from the releasing steam.

Meals in an Instant
• ELECTRIC PRESSURE COOKER •

Bacon-Braised Mixed Greens
Geneva Rogers
Gillette, WY

One day I got carried away with how fresh and good everything looked at a roadside stand...what to do with all these greens? This easy recipe came to the rescue.

4 slices bacon, diced
1/2 onion, diced
2 cloves garlic, pressed
1/8 t. sugar
1 bunch kale, chopped
1 bunch collard greens, chopped

1 bunch mustard greens, chopped
3 c. chicken broth
2 to 3 T. cider vinegar
salt and pepper to taste

Add bacon and onion to a 5-quart electric pressure cooker; turn heat to medium-high. Cook for about 3 minutes, until bacon is lightly crisp. Stir in garlic and sugar. Add greens and broth, pushing down until greens wilt enough to fit into pot. Close and lock lid. When high pressure is reached, reduce heat as low as possible while still maintaining high pressure. Set timer and cook for 8 minutes; turn off heat and let stand for 6 minutes. Open pressure cooker using quick release method; stir but do not drain. Stir in vinegar; season with salt and pepper. Serves 6.

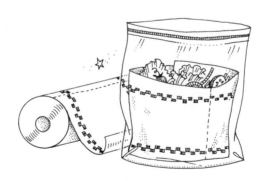

Keep leafy greens farmstand-fresh for up to a week. After you bring them home, rinse greens in cool water, wrap in paper towels and slip into a plastic zipping bag with several small holes cut in it. Tuck the bag in the fridge's crisper bin... ready to use when you are!

Chicken & Wild Rice

Patti Wafford
Mount Vernon, TX

One of the first recipes I tried in my electric pressure cooker...it was a hit with my family!

3-1/2 c. chicken broth
2 c. boneless, skinless chicken
  breasts, cubed
1 c. long-cooking wild rice,
  uncooked
2 c. long-cooking brown rice,
  uncooked

2 T. butter or olive oil
2 T. soy sauce
salt and pepper to taste
Optional: 1 c. frozen peas, frozen
  chopped broccoli or frozen
  sliced carrots

Add broth to a 5-quart electric pressure cooker. Push sauté button and allow to heat; add remaining ingredients and stir well. Close and lock lid. Bring up to high pressure using manual setting; push multi-grain button. Set timer and cook for 35 minutes. Open pressure cooker using quick release method. Stir before serving. Makes 4 to 6 servings.

Rewrite: Better safe than sorry! Do not leave instant pot on stovetop, and do not release pressure under a cupboard.

Meals in an Instant
• ELECTRIC PRESSURE COOKER •

Chicken "Anything"

Jane Martin
Havre de Grace, MD

Toss a whole chicken in the pressure cooker for 35 minutes, and you've got dinner for tonight! Or, chop or shred it and freeze for future meals. The broth left behind is divine! You can use any seasoning you like, keeping in mind that it seasons the broth more than the chicken.

1 c. chicken broth
4 to 5-lb. whole chicken
salt and pepper to taste

Optional: Herbs de Provence
to taste

Add broth to a 6-quart electric pressure cooker. Remove giblets and neck from chicken; place chicken in pressure cooker, breast-side up. Season as desired. Close and lock lid. Set timer and cook for 35 to 40 minutes, depending on size of chicken. Open pressure cooker using natural release method. Chicken should be falling-apart tender; remove to a large platter with tongs. Serve as desired; reserve broth to use as desired. Makes 6 to 8 servings.

Herbes de Provence is a special herb blend that's perfect with roast meats. It can contain as many as a dozen different herbs...look for it in the spice aisle. Or, mix up a simple version with 3 tablespoons each dried oregano, savory and thyme, 2 tablespoons dried lavender, and one teaspoon each dried basil, rosemary and sage.

Meatloaf & Mashed Potatoes

Cheryl Culver
Coyle, OK

All in one pot, simple, easy and ready in less than half the time of cooking it all on the stovetop or oven. This is dinner made simple and tasty!

2 lbs. ground beef
1 c. Italian-seasoned dry
   bread crumbs
1 egg, beaten
1/3 c. catsup or barbecue sauce
2 T. garlic, minced
2 T. dried, minced onion
2 t. dried parsley
1 to 2 t. Worcestershire sauce

1 c. water
2 lbs. Yukon Gold potatoes,
   cubed
Optional: additional catsup or
   barbecue sauce
1/2 c. half-and-half
1/2 c. chicken broth
2 T. butter
salt and pepper to taste

In a large bowl, combine beef, bread crumbs, egg, catsup or barbecue sauce, garlic, onion, parsley and Worcestershire sauce. Mix well, using your hands. Transfer to a disposable foil loaf pan (or shape a "pan" from heavy-duty foil); set aside. Arrange potatoes evenly in a 6-quart electric pressure cooker; add water. Set a rack or trivet over potatoes; set meatloaf on top. Close and lock lid; set on high pressure manually for 25 minutes. Open pressure cooker using quick release method. Remove meatloaf in pan. Top with a little additional catsup or sauce, if desired; place under the broiler for a few minutes, until caramelized, if desired. Add half-and-half, broth, butter and seasonings to potatoes in pressure cooker; mash until creamy. Serves 4 to 6.

For heavenly mashed potatoes, mix just until all ingredients are blended...don't over-mix.

Beef & Pasta Ragu

Virginia Butterfield
Cranberry Twp., PA

This is delicious, super quick & easy. Serve with a chopped salad and Italian dressing. Any leftovers are good spooned into individual ramekins and baked with a little extra sauce and some cheese on top.

1 to 1-1/2 T. olive oil
3/4 c. onion, finely chopped
1 green pepper, chopped
1 T. Italian seasoning
1-1/2 lbs. lean ground beef

12-oz. pkg. penne pasta,
   uncooked
2-1/4 c. water
5-1/2 c. pasta sauce

Set a 6-quart electric pressure cooker to sauté. Add oil; sauté onion and pepper until onion is translucent. Sprinkle with seasoning. Add beef and brown, stirring frequently; drain. Spread uncooked pasta over beef mixture. Pour in water; it should nearly cover the pasta. Spoon in pasta sauce on top. Close and lock lid. Cook on high pressure for 6 minutes. Open pressure cooker using quick release method; stir well and serve. Makes 6 to 8 servings.

A zesty tossed salad is right at home alongside pasta dishes. Toss together mixed greens, ripe cherry tomatoes and thinly sliced red onion in a salad bowl. Whisk together 1/4 cup each of balsamic vinegar and olive oil, drizzle over the salad and serve.

Cheeseburger Macaroni

Nancy Kailihiwa
Wheatland, CA

I love my pressure cooker and am always looking for simple meals to make in minutes. This is one our family loves. You can substitute any cheese combinations you like.

2 lbs. lean ground beef
1/2 c. onion
1-1/2 t. garlic, minced
4 c. elbow macaroni, uncooked
32-oz. pkg. beef broth
1/4 c. butter
1/2 c. sour cream
1/2 c. milk

Optional: 1 c. canned nacho
cheese sauce
2 c. shredded sharp Cheddar
cheese
1 c. shredded Mexican-blend
cheese
1/2 c. shredded Parmesan cheese

Cook beef, onion and garlic in a skillet over medium heat; drain. Meanwhile, combine macaroni and broth in a 6-quart electric pressure cooker. Close and lock lid; set to high and cook for 6 minutes. Let stand for 5 minutes; open pressure cooker using quick release method. Stir in butter, sour cream, milk and cheese sauce, if using. Add cheeses and stir until melted. Add beef mixture and stir well. Serves 8.

Hamburger or hot dog buns make the yummiest garlic bread. Spread bun halves with softened butter, add garlic salt to taste and pop under the broiler until toasty and golden.

Spaghetti & Meatballs in a Pot

Linda Peterson
Mason, MI

This dish tastes even better the next day!

3-1/2 c. water, divided
14-oz. pkg. frozen meatballs
24-oz. jar spaghetti sauce

16-oz. pkg. spaghetti, uncooked
   and broken into thirds

Add 1/2 cup water to a 5 to 6-quart electric pressure cooker. Add frozen meatballs, spaghetti sauce, uncooked spaghetti and remaining water; stir gently. Close and lock lid; close pressure valve. Set timer and cook at high pressure for 3 minutes. Open pressure cooker using a 5-minute natural release method, then a quick release. Stir gently to break up any clumps of spaghetti. Serves 4 to 6.

Choosing a new electric pressure cooker? The 6-quart size is perfect for families and will accommodate most recipes. If you already have a 5-quart, it'll be fine with most recipes calling for a 6-quart. An 8-quart model is also fine for most 6-quart recipes, and will allow enough room to make a double batch.

Chicken & Rice Burrito Bowls

Vickie
Gooseberry Patch

Southwestern-style comfort food, ready in no time at all!

1-1/2 T. oil
3/4 c. onion, diced
2 cloves garlic, minced
1 T. chili powder
1-1/2 t. ground cumin
1 c. chicken broth, divided
1-1/2 lbs. boneless, skinless
  chicken thighs, cut into
  1-inch cubes

salt and pepper to taste
15-1/2 oz. can black beans,
  drained and rinsed
1 c. frozen corn
16-oz. jar salsa
1 c. long-cooking rice, uncooked
Optional: shredded sharp
  Cheddar cheese

Set a 5-quart electric pressure cooker to sauté; add oil. Sauté onion and garlic for about 4 minutes, until softened. Stir in chili powder and cumin; cook until fragrant, about 30 seconds. Add 1/4 cup broth and simmer for one minute, stirring to loosen any browned bits in the bottom of pot. Turn off sauté setting. Season chicken cubes with salt and pepper. Add chicken, beans, corn and salsa to pressure cooker; stir. Sprinkle uncooked rice on top; drizzle with remaining broth. Do not stir. Close and lock lid; set pressure manually to high and cook for 10 minutes. Open pressure cooker using quick release method; stir gently. To serve, divide among bowls; top with cheese, if desired. Serves 4 to 6.

Mix up your own chili powder blend! Fill a shaker with 2 teaspoons each garlic powder and ground cumin and one teaspoon each of cayenne pepper, paprika and oregano. It's easily adjusted to your family's liking.

Meals in an Instant
• ELECTRIC PRESSURE COOKER •

Charro Beans

Tonya Sheppard
Galveston, TX

I like to fix these flavorful beans for our backyard cookouts.
No need to watch a pot on the stovetop!

4 c. water
2 c. dried pinto beans, rinsed
    and sorted
1 onion, chopped
1/2 c. fresh cilantro, or to taste,
    coarsely chopped
1 jalapeño pepper, minced
4 cloves garlic, minced

2 t. tomato or chicken bouillon
    granules
2 t. vegetable bouillon granules
1/2 t. chili powder
1/2 t. ground cumin
1/2 t. paprika
1/2 t. pepper
Optional: 1/2 c. salsa

Combine all ingredients in a 4-quart electric pressure cooker; stir well.
Close and lock lid. Select bean/chili function; set timer and cook for
45 minutes. Open pressure cooker using natural release method. Stir
before serving. Makes 8 servings.

Turn Charro Beans into a delicious bean dip! After cooking,
scoop the beans into a casserole dish and mash until smooth.
Top generously with Cheddar Jack cheese and broil until
cheese is bubbly. Serve with tortilla chips.

Southwestern-Style Black Beans & Bacon

Connie Hilty
Pearland, TX

We like these beans with a big pan of buttered cornbread. Leftovers are great for lunch, stuffed into pita pockets.

1 lb. dried black beans, rinsed
    and sorted
5 slices bacon, chopped
2 T. olive oil
3/4 c. onion, finely chopped
1 green pepper, chopped
3 cloves garlic, minced

2 t. ground cumin
4-oz. can diced roasted green
    chiles
15-oz. can tomato sauce
2-1/2 c. water
1/2 c. water
salt and pepper to taste

Place beans in a deep bowl; add enough water to cover by 2 inches. Soak for 8 hours or overnight. Drain; rinse and set aside. In a 5-quart electric pressure cooker on medium heat, cook bacon just until crisp. With bacon still in the pot, use paper towels to blot up excess drippings. Add oil, onion, green pepper and garlic; stir to coat. Cook until softened, 3 to 4 minutes. Sprinkle with cumin; add undrained chiles, tomato sauce and water. Stir in beans; bring to a rolling boil. Close and lock lid; set heat to high. Once high pressure is reached, reduce heat as low as possible, still maintaining high pressure. Set timer and cook for 7 minutes. Open pressure cooker using natural release method; let stand for 15 minutes. If too much liquid is still in the pot, simmer, uncovered, to desired consistency. Season with salt and pepper. Serves 6.

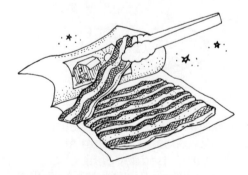

Save time on recipes that use bacon, but not the drippings...just substitute ready-to-use cooked bacon.

Meals in an Instant
• ELECTRIC PRESSURE COOKER •

Mexican Rice

Liz Plotnick-Snay
Gooseberry Patch

The perfect side for all your south-of-the-border favorites! Easily doubled too.

1 T. oil, or more as needed
1/2 c. onion, finely chopped
2 to 3 cloves garlic, minced
1 c. long-cooking rice, uncooked
1-1/2 c. chicken broth

1/2 c. tomato sauce
1/4 t. ground cumin
1/8 t. cayenne pepper
1 t. salt

Set a 4-quart electric pressure cooker to sauté and adjust to medium. Add oil and onion; cook and stir for 4 to 5 minutes, until softened. Add garlic and cook until fragrant, about 30 seconds. Add uncooked rice; stir until golden and coated with oil. Add broth; stir up any browned bits on bottom of pot. Stir in tomato sauce and seasonings. Close and lock lid. Set pressure manually to high; cook for 7 minutes. Open pressure cooker using quick release method. Stir before serving. Serves 4.

For a fantastic lunch, make a bowl meal with Mexican leftovers! Layer seasoned rice, refried beans and sliced roast beef or chicken in a bowl. Microwave until hot, then garnish with shredded lettuce, diced onion and a dollop of sour cream.

Baby Back Pork Ribs

Cheryl Culver
Coyle, OK

These are the most delicious, juicy baby back ribs from the pressure cooker you will ever taste! The recipe can be doubled by wrapping the second rack of ribs around the first. Double the spices, but keep the same amount of liquid underneath.

1/4 c. brown sugar, packed
2 T. chili powder
2 t. dried parsley
1 t. ground cumin
1 t. garlic powder
1 t. onion powder
1 t. salt
1 t. pepper

1/4 t. cayenne pepper
3-lb. rack pork baby back ribs,
   cut into serving-size pieces
1 c. water
1/2 c. cider vinegar
Optional: 1/4 t. smoke-flavored
   cooking sauce
1/2 c. barbecue sauce

Combine brown sugar and seasonings in a cup; rub all over ribs and set aside. Place a rack or trivet in a 6-quart electric pressure cooker. Place ribs on rack, standing on their side, wrapping around the inside of the pot. Pour in water, vinegar and smoke-flavored sauce, if using, being careful to not rinse off any of seasoning rub. Close and lock lid. Select meat function; cook for 55 minutes. Open pressure cooker using natural release method for 10 minutes; use quick release for remaining pressure. Carefully remove ribs to an aluminum foil-lined baking sheet. Brush with barbecue sauce. Place under the broiler for 5 minutes, watching closely to avoid burning. Makes 4 to 6 servings.

For recipes that you make often, mix up several small bags of the seasoning blend. Label with the recipe's name and tuck in the cupboard...a terrific time-saver for future meals!

Classic Potato Salad

Kelly Alderson
Erie, PA

Everyone's favorite mayonnaise potato salad...just like Grandma used to make, only a little quicker! If you like, add a few chopped hard-boiled eggs. May be made up to a day ahead.

1-1/2 c. water
3 lbs. Yukon Gold or redskin
   potatoes, halved
3/4 to 1 c. mayonnaise,
   as needed
2 T. cider vinegar

2 t. Dijon mustard
1 t. salt
pepper to taste
4 green onions, thinly sliced
3 stalks celery, diced

Place a rack or trivet in a 5-quart electric pressure cooker; add water. Place potatoes in a steamer basket and set in pot; water should not touch potatoes. Cover and lock lid; set to high. When high pressure is reached, reduce heat as low as possible while still maintaining high pressure. Set timer and cook for 7 minutes. Open pressure cooker using natural release method; let stand for 15 minutes. Transfer potatoes to a bowl; cover loosely and chill until cooled. In a large serving bowl, whisk together mayonnaise, vinegar, mustard and seasonings. Add potatoes, onions and celery; toss until well coated. Cover and chill before serving. Makes 6 to 8 servings.

Unlike slow cookers, electric pressure cookers need more liquid to work properly. Most recipes will call for at least one cup of liquid such as water or broth, but if yours doesn't, be sure to add it. The exception is cakes and other items made in a separate pan.

Ham with Honey-Mustard Glaze

Dale Duncan
Waterloo, IA

A meltingly tender ham everyone loves! Plan on about 1/3 pound sliced ham per person.

1 to 1-1/2 c. sparkling apple
  cider or ginger ale
1/3 c. honey Dijon mustard
1/4 c. brown sugar, packed

1/8 t. ground cloves
2-1/2 to 4-lb. fully cooked
  boneless ham

Place a trivet or rack in a 6-quart electric pressure cooker. Add enough cider or ginger ale to just reach the bottom of the rack; set aside. In a small bowl, whisk together mustard, brown sugar and cloves; brush over ham. Place ham in a steamer basket, fat-side up. Set basket in pressure cooker; make sure it does not exceed the 2/3 full level. Close and lock lid; set heat to high. When high pressure is reached, reduce heat as low possible while still maintaining high pressure. Set timer and cook for 11 minutes for a 2-1/2 to 3-pound ham, or 15 minutes for a larger ham. Open pressure cooker using natural release method; let stand for 15 minutes. Transfer ham to a platter. Cover with aluminum foil; let stand at least 15 minutes before slicing. Serves 4 to 10, depending on size of ham.

Homemade coleslaw is scrumptious with baked ham.
Blend 1/2 cup mayonnaise, 2 tablespoons milk, one tablespoon
vinegar and 1/2 teaspoon sugar. Add a bag of shredded
coleslaw mix and toss to coat. For a yummy variation,
toss in some pineapple tidbits. Chill before serving.

Meals in an Instant
• ELECTRIC PRESSURE COOKER •

Stewed Fruit

Kendall Hale
Lynn, MA

My mother used to make a similar mixture of dried fruit to serve at Christmas with baked ham or turkey. This is similar, but so much quicker! It's also delicious over ice cream. Mix & match dried fruit as you like...apples, pears and peaches are great too.

3 c. Zinfandel wine or grape juice
1 c. water
3/4 c. sugar
4-inch cinnamon stick
1/2 to 3/4 vanilla bean

12-oz. pkg. dried apricots
12-oz. pkg. dried prunes
12-oz. pkg. dried figs
1/2 c. mixed dried tart cherries
   and golden raisins

In a 5-quart electric pressure cooker, combine wine or juice, water, sugar and cinnamon stick. Split vanilla bean nearly in half lengthwise; add to mixture. Bring to a boil on high heat. Cook and stir until sugar dissolves; simmer for 2 minutes. Add fruits and return to a boil. Still on high heat, close and lock lid. When high pressure is reached, reduce heat as low as possible while still maintaining high pressure. Set timer and cook for 8 minutes. Open pressure cooker using natural release method; let stand for 15 minutes. Remove cinnamon stick and vanilla bean. Transfer fruit with stewing liquid to a glass bowl; cover and chill at least 4 hours. Serve chilled. May keep refrigerated up to 4 days. Makes 8 servings.

For a simple yet elegant dessert in a jiffy,
spoon Stewed Fruit over slices of angel food cake.

One-Pot Pork & Cabbage Dinner

Lori Britt
Montgomery, IL

My sister used to make this dish in a stockpot on the stove. It smelled so good when we came home from school. Years later, I made it in my stovetop pressure cooker to save time. Now I use my electric pressure cooker, and it's so easy...I love it! Add a loaf of crusty bread and dinner is served.

4 to 6 potatoes, peeled and
   quartered
2 onions, cut into wide strips
1/2 lb. baby carrots
2 14-1/2 oz. cans cut green
   beans, drained

1-1/2 lb. smoked pork shoulder
   butt, quartered and sliced
   1/2-inch thick
1 head cabbage, cut into wedges
1 c. water
2 T. garlic bread seasoning

In a 6-quart electric pressure cooker, layer potatoes, onions, carrots, green beans and pork; place cabbage on top. Add water; sprinkle with seasoning. Cover and lock lid. Set on high pressure using manual setting, 10 minutes. Open pressure cooker using quick release method. Makes 4 servings.

A splash of cider vinegar adds zing to any cabbage dish.

Homemade Cinnamon Applesauce

Carol Lytle
Columbus, OH

Applesauce in a pressure cooker takes just a few minutes! Use all of one type of apple, like a firm cooking apple, or a combination of tart and softer sweet apples.

6 to 7 Fuji or Golden Delicious
   apples, peeled, cored,
   and cut into chunks
1/4 c. brown sugar, packed

1-1/2 t. cinnamon
1 c. unsweetened apple juice
   or water
1 T. lemon juice

Combine all ingredients in a 5-quart electric pressure cooker. Close and lock lid; set heat to high. When high pressure is reached, reduce heat as low as possible while still maintaining high pressure. Set timer and cook for 2 minutes. Open pressure cooker using natural release method; let stand for 15 minutes. Using a wooden spoon or a potato masher, mash apples to desired consistency, breaking up any large chunks. If a smoother texture is desired, purée applesauce right in the pot, using an immersion blender. Transfer to a covered container; keep refrigerated up to 5 days. Makes about 4 cups.

Head out to a pick-your-own apple orchard for a day of fresh-air fun. The kids will love it, and you'll come home with bushels of the best-tasting apples! McIntosh apples are perfect for applesauce because they are juicy and break down easily.

Sausage & Cavatappi with Spinach

Sonia Daily
Rochester, MI

My go-to weeknight pressure cooker dinner! A great recipe that cooks so fast. Serve with a tossed salad and you are good to go!

1 T. olive oil
1 onion, minced
1/2 t. salt
1 lb. sweet Italian pork sausage
    links, each cut into 5 pieces
3 cloves garlic, minced
1/2 c. sun-dried tomatoes,
    finely chopped

4 c. cavatappi or penne pasta,
    uncooked
2 c. chicken broth
1 c. milk
1/2 c. grated Parmesan cheese
5-oz. pkg. baby spinach
salt and pepper to taste

Set a 6-quart electric pressure cooker on sauté. Add oil; heat until shimmering. Add onion and 1/2 teaspoon salt; cook until softened, about 5 minutes. Add sausage; cook until browned. Stir in garlic; cook for about 15 seconds. Add tomatoes, uncooked pasta and broth. Cover and lock lid. Set timer and cook for 4 minutes on high pressure. Open pressure cooker using quick release method. Add milk, cheese and spinach; stir until warmed through and spinach is wilted. Season with salt and pepper. Serves 6.

Make a chopped salad in seconds...no cutting board needed! Add all the salad fixings except salad dressing to a big bowl, then roll a pizza cutter back & forth over them. Drizzle with dressing and enjoy your salad.

Italian-Style Braised Zucchini

Sarah Oravecz
Gooseberry Patch

This recipe is perfect for when your garden just won't stop producing those oversized zucchini! Mix & match with yellow squash or other summer squash too.

2 T. olive oil
1 c. onion, chopped
2 cloves garlic, pressed
1 lb. zucchini, sliced
    1/2-inch thick
1 c. canned Italian-seasoned
    diced tomatoes

1/4 c. vegetable broth or water
pepper to taste
1 T. basil pesto sauce
salt to taste
Garnish: grated Parmesan
    cheese

In a 5-quart electric pressure cooker pot, heat oil over medium-high heat. Add onion for about 3 minutes, just until soft. Add garlic; cook and stir for 30 seconds. Add zucchini, tomatoes with juice and broth or water; bring to a boil. Season with pepper. Close and lock lid; set heat to high. When high pressure is reached, reduce heat as low as possible while still maintaining high pressure. Set timer and cook for 2 minutes. Turn off pressure cooker; let stand up to 2 minutes. Open pressure cooker using quick release method. Stir in pesto; season with salt. Serve warm or at room temperature, sprinkled with Parmesan cheese. Makes 4 to 6 servings.

Add texture and flavor to tender vegetable dishes with a crunchy crumb topping. Sauté soft bread crumbs in butter or olive oil until crisp and golden...sprinkle with chopped herbs for extra flavor.

Simple Swiss Steak

Jenita Davison
La Plata, MO

My electric pressure cooker turns this into a quick, delicious meal! It makes a scrumptious tomato gravy that we like to spoon over mashed potatoes.

4 4 to 6-oz. tenderized beef
    round steaks
1/4 c. all-purpose flour
garlic salt and pepper to taste
1 T. oil
8-oz. can Italian tomato sauce
1 c. water

1/2 onion, diced
1/4 green pepper, diced
2 to 4 mushrooms, chopped
1 stalk celery, diced
1 t. garlic, minced
Optional: 2 T. cornstarch

Dredge steaks in flour; season with garlic salt and pepper. Set a 5-quart electric pressure cooker on sauté; heat oil. Add steaks and brown on both sides; drain. In a bowl, combine tomato sauce, water, vegetables and garlic; spoon over steaks. Cover and lock lid. Cook on high pressure for 20 minutes. Open pressure cooker using natural release; remove steaks to a plate. If a thicker gravy consistency is desired, mix together 2 tablespoons of hot cooking liquid with cornstarch; stir back into liquid in pressure cooker. Turn to sauté; simmer for one to 2 minutes, until thickened. Spoon gravy over steaks to serve. Makes 4 servings.

If you have a small family, a 3-quart pressure cooker may be right for you. Recipes created for 6-quart pressure cookers can usually be adapted, dividing only the solid ingredients in half. Liquid ingredients and cooking time will remain unchanged. A little experimenting will ensure picture-perfect results.

Meals in an Instant
• ELECTRIC PRESSURE COOKER •

Buttermilk Mashed Potatoes

Nancy Wise
Little Rock, AR

Buttermilk gives a tang to good ol' mashed potatoes that my family loves. When mashing, the more milk, the fluffier the potatoes!

5 to 6 russet potatoes, peeled and
    cut into 2-inch cubes
3/4 t. salt
3 T. butter, sliced

3/4 c. buttermilk, or more
    as needed
salt and pepper to taste

Place potatoes in a 5-quart electric pressure cooker; add just enough water to cover potatoes and mix in salt. Close and lock lid; set heat to high. When high pressure is reached, reduce heat as low as possible and still maintain high pressure. Set timer and cook for 6 minutes. Open pressure cooker using quick release method; potatoes should be fork-tender. Drain in a colander; transfer to a deep bowl. Mash potatoes with a potato masher or beat with an electric mixer on low speed. Mix in butter until melted; add buttermilk. Beat to desired consistency, adding more buttermilk, one tablespoon at a time, if needed. Season with salt and pepper. Makes 4 to 6 servings.

The ultimate comfort food...place a scoop of mashed potatoes in the center of a soup bowl, then ladle hearty stew all around.

Mediterranean Chicken

JoAnn
Gooseberry Patch

We were bored with the same old chicken recipes, then I found this one...bored no more! The tender chicken with its lemony sauce is delicious served over angel hair pasta.

4 to 6 chicken thighs
salt and pepper to taste
1 T. olive oil
3 T. butter, divided
1/2 onion, minced
1/2 c. chicken broth

1/4 c. white wine or
  chicken broth
1 lemon, thinly sliced
1 c. pitted Kalamata olives
1-1/2 t. lemon zest
1/4 c. lemon juice

Season chicken with salt and pepper; set aside. Add oil and one tablespoon butter to a 4-quart pressure cooker. Add chicken, a few pieces at a time; cook for 2 to 3 minutes on each side, until golden. Remove chicken to a plate; add remaining butter, onion, broth and wine or broth. Set timer and cook for 2 to 3 minutes, until liquid cooks down by half. Add remaining ingredients; arrange chicken on top. Cover and lock lid. Cook on high setting for 20 minutes. Open pressure cooker using quick release method. Serve chicken topped with sauce from pressure cooker. Makes 4 to 6 servings.

For the freshest flavor, store olive oil in the fridge...just pour a little into a small cruet for everyday use. Olive oil thickens when chilled, but will thin quickly at room temperature.

Chicken Piccata with Artichokes

Marlene Darnell
Newport Beach, CA

Do you want a dish to impress guests? Combine the chicken and marinade by mid-afternoon, then cook up this savory, elegant dish in no time at all. Serve over steamed rice.

4 T. olive oil, divided
1/2 c. lemon juice
salt and pepper to taste
8 boneless, skinless chicken
   thighs
salt and pepper to taste
2 T. butter

2 T. shallot, minced
3/4 c. chicken broth
3 T. capers, drained and rinsed
14-oz. can quartered artichokes,
   drained
zest of 1 lemon

In a shallow bowl, combine 2 tablespoons oil, lemon juice, salt and pepper; stir well. Add chicken; turn to coat all sides. Cover and refrigerate for 2 to 4 hours. Transfer chicken to a plate, reserving marinade. Bring marinade to a boil in a small saucepan; set aside. Pat chicken dry with paper towels; season lightly with salt and pepper. In a 5-quart electric pressure cooker, heat butter and remaining oil over medium-high heat until sizzling. Working in batches, add chicken and cook until golden, about 3 minutes on each side. Transfer chicken to a plate. Add shallots and cook for 2 minutes. Add broth and reserved marinade; scrape up any browned bits from bottom of pot. Return chicken and any juices from plate to pot; sprinkle with capers. Close and lock lid; set heat to high. When high pressure is reached, reduce heat as low as possible while still maintaining high pressure. Set timer and cook for 8 minutes. Open pressure cooker using quick release method. Stir in artichokes and lemon zest; stir until warmed through. Serve chicken topped with artichokes and sauce from pressure cooker. Makes 4 servings.

For hearty salads in a snap, keep unopened cans of diced tomatoes, marinated artichokes, black olives and white beans in the fridge. They'll be chilled and ready to toss with fresh greens at a moment's notice.

Cider Mill Brisket

Regina Vining
Warwick, RI

This brisket tastes even better the second day! Prepare and refrigerate, then rewarm before serving time. Serve with mashed potatoes or egg noodles, with the horseradish sauce on the side.

4-lb. center-cut beef brisket,
   quartered and fat trimmed
1 t. salt
1/4 t. pepper
2 T. olive oil
2 yellow onions, sliced
   1/2-inch thick

12-oz. bottle hard cider or
   1-1/2 c. apple cider
1 c. apple cider
1/2 t. dried rosemary
1/2 t. dried thyme

Season brisket all over with salt and pepper; set aside. In a 6-quart electric pressure cooker, heat oil over medium-high heat until very hot. Working in batches, add one to 2 pieces of brisket to pot and brown, about 3 minutes per side. Transfer browned pieces to a plate until all are done. Add onions to drippings in pot; cook for 2 to 3 minutes. Using a slotted spoon, transfer 2/3 of the onions to a bowl. Stack brisket pieces in pot, spooning some onions in between pieces and spreading remaining onions on top. Add ciders and herbs. Close and lock lid. Set heat to high. When high pressure is reached, reduce heat as low as possible while still on high pressure. Set timer and cook for 60 minutes. Open pressure cooker using quick release method. Transfer brisket pieces to a cutting board; slice across the grain, about 1/3 inch thick. Arrange slices in a casserole dish; spoon cooking liquid and onions over top and between the slices. Cover and bake at 350 degrees for 30 minutes. Serve with Creamy Horseradish Sauce. Serves 8.

Creamy Horseradish Sauce:

1/2 c. sour cream
1 t. cider vinegar

1/8 t. sugar
2 to 3 T. prepared horseradish

Combine mayonnaise, vinegar, sugar and horseradish to taste. Cover and chill.

Meals in an Instant
• ELECTRIC PRESSURE COOKER •

Smashed Red Potatoes

Michelle Kerns
Saint Joseph, MI

*Grated Parmesan cheese is also a good addition to this recipe.
You can even make a loaded potato version and add crumbled
bacon, green onions and Cheddar cheese. Yum!*

3 lbs. redskin potatoes, cut into
   2-inch chunks
2 c. water
2 t. salt
1/4 c. butter, softened
3/4 c. milk, or to taste, warmed

1/4 c. sour cream
2 T. fresh parsley, minced,
   or 1 T. dried parsley
1 T. onion, minced
1/2 t. garlic powder
salt and pepper to taste

Add potatoes, water and salt to a 5-quart electric pressure cooker.
Close and lock lid. Cook on manual high pressure for 9 minutes. Open
pressure cooker using quick release method; drain potatoes well and
return inner pot to pressure cooker. With pressure cooker set to keep
warm, add butter. When butter is melted, return potatoes to pot; mash
lightly with a potato masher. Add just enough warm milk to make
potatoes creamy but not soupy. Stir in remaining ingredients. Makes
5 to 6 servings.

Potatoes & Green Beans

Kathy Van Daalen
New Smyrna Beach, FL

My kids love their veggies fixed this way!

4 potatoes, peeled and cubed
1 lb. fresh green beans, trimmed
1 onion, sliced

5 slices bacon, chopped
2 c. chicken broth
salt and pepper to taste

Combine all ingredients in a 4-quart electric pressure cooker. Close and
lock lid. Set timer and cook for 15 minutes on high pressure. Open
pressure cooker using quick release method. Drain and serve. Makes
6 servings.

Roasted Eggplant & Tomato Pasta Sauce

Barb Bargdill
Gooseberry Patch

Both purple and white eggplants work well in this savory sauce.
It's delicious served over penne pasta, topped with grated
Parmesan cheese and sliced black olives.

1-1/2 lbs. eggplant, halved
1/2 to 1 t. salt
1/2 c. olive oil, divided
3 cloves garlic, peeled
2 onions, finely chopped
3/4 lb. sliced mushrooms
6-oz. can tomato paste

28-oz. can whole plum tomatoes, crushed
1/2 c. red wine or water
1 T. dried parsley
1-1/2 t. dried oregano
pepper to taste

Sprinkle cut sides of eggplant with salt; drain on paper towels for 30 minutes and rinse. Brush some of the oil over a baking sheet. Brush eggplant halves and garlic cloves with oil; arrange place on baking sheet. Bake at 400 degrees for about 20 minutes, until tender. Let cool; peel eggplant and coarsely chop. Press garlic into a paste; set aside. In a 5-quart electric pressure cooker, heat remaining oil over medium-high heat. Add onions and cook for about 3 minutes. Add mushrooms; cook until they release their their liquid. Add tomato paste; cook and stir for one minute. Add tomatoes with juice, wine or water and seasonings; bring to a boil. Stir in eggplant and garlic. Close and lock lid. Set heat to high. Bring pressure cooker to high pressure; reduce heat as low as possible while still on high pressure. Set timer and cook for 8 minutes. Open pressure cooker using natural release method; let stand for 15 minutes. Sauce may be served immediately, or cooled completely and transferred to a covered container. Refrigerate up to 3 days or freeze up to 4 months. Makes about 5 cups, enough for 1-1/2 pounds cooked pasta.

Meals in an Instant
• ELECTRIC PRESSURE COOKER •

Summer Succotash

Melanie Lowe
Dover, DE

We love this easy combination of all the fresh vegetables from our garden! In wintertime, it's almost as good made with frozen corn and winter squash instead of yellow. Delicious with grilled or roasted meats.

3 ears sweet corn, husked
1 T. olive oil
1 c. onion, diced
1 to 2 cloves garlic, minced
1 c. fresh or frozen baby
    lima beans
2 to 3 zucchini, cut in half
    lengthwise and sliced

1 to 2 yellow squash,
    cut into chunks
2 roma tomatoes, diced
1/2 c. chicken broth
1 to 2 t. dried thyme
2 T. fresh parsley, chopped
salt and pepper to taste
red wine vinegar to taste

With a sharp knife, cut off corn kernels. Scrape cobs using the dull edge of the knife to extract the "milk" and additional pulp; there should be about 2 cups. Set aside. In a 5-quart electric pressure cooker, heat oil over medium-high heat. Add onion and garlic; cook for about 2 minutes, just until tender. Add corn, beans, squash, tomatoes, broth and thyme. Close and lock lid. Set heat to high. When pressure cooker comes to high pressure, reduce heat as low as possible while still on high pressure. Set timer and cook for 2 minutes. Open pressure cooker using quick release method; stir in seasonings. Drizzle lightly with vinegar. Makes 4 servings.

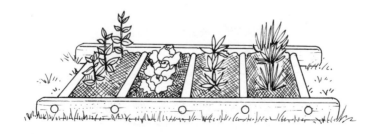

He who shares the joy in what he's grown
Spreads joy abroad and doubles his own.
– Anonymous

Risotto with Italian Sausage & Kale

Kelley Nicholson
Gooseberry Patch

Zesty Italian flavors make this a popular choice for casual weeknight dinners. A tossed green salad and some crusty bread round out the meal nicely.

1 T. olive oil
1/2 lb. sweet or hot Italian
   ground pork sausage
1 T. butter
1/2 c. onion, chopped
3 c. fresh kale, chopped
1/2 t. salt

1/4 t. red pepper flakes
1 c. arborio rice, uncooked
1/3 c. white wine or broth
2-1/4 c. chicken or vegetable
   broth
2/3 c. shredded Parmesan
   cheese, divided

In a 5-quart electric pressure cooker, heat oil over medium-high heat until very hot. Add sausage and cook until browned. Drain, reserving one tablespoon drippings in pot; add butter and onion. Cook until onion is softened, about 3 minutes. Stir in kale and seasonings. Add rice; stir to coat. Pour in 1/3 cup wine or broth; scrape up browned bits from bottom of pot. Stir in 2-1/4 cups broth. Close and lock the lid. Set heat to high; bring to high pressure. Reduce heat as low as possible while still maintaining high pressure. Set timer and cook for 7 minutes. Open pressure cooker using quick release method. If mixture is too soupy or rice is not tender, cook on medium-high heat, uncovered, for one to 2 minutes, stirring constantly. Stir in 1/3 cup cheese; season with more salt if desired. Serve at once in shallow bowls with remaining cheese. Makes 2 to 3 servings.

Oops! If you accidentally poured water directly into the pressure cooker without adding the inner pot first, unplug it, empty it and allow it to dry completely before using it again.

Garlicky White Beans & Sage

April Jacobs
Loveland, CO

You'll definitely want to use fresh sage in this recipe to enjoy its savory flavor. Store fresh sage leaves in the refrigerator in a plastic bag, or you may wrap them in a damp paper towel; they will usually last for 3 to 4 days.

1 lb. dried Great Northern beans,
   rinsed and sorted
2 14-oz. cans chicken broth
6 T. olive oil, divided
1 onion, quartered
6 fresh sage leaves

12 cloves garlic, or to taste,
   minced
salt and pepper to taste
Optional: 2 T. fresh parsley,
   chopped

Place beans in a deep bowl; add enough water to cover by 2 inches. Soak for 8 hours or overnight. Drain; rinse and transfer beans to a 5-quart electric pressure cooker. Add broth and enough water so that liquid is one inch above beans. Drizzle in one tablespoon oil; add onion and sage. Close and lock lid. Set heat to high; bring to high pressure. Turn down heat as low as possible while still on high pressure. Set timer and cook for 7 minutes. Open cooker using natural release method; let stand for 10 minutes. Drain, discarding onion and sage. Gently heat 4 tablespoons oil in a skillet over low heat. Add garlic; cook and stir until lightly golden, one to 2 minutes. Stir oil mixture into beans; season with salt and pepper. At serving time, drizzle beans with remaining oil; sprinkle with parsley, if desired. Makes 8 servings.

Peeled garlic in a jiffy! Lay a silicone hot pad on the counter, fold it over your garlic clove and give it a whack. Your garlic will be peeled and ready to chop.

Pork Chop, Kraut & Potato Dinner

Leota Hall
Lincoln, NE

This was always a favorite of my kids then and now since they have grown up. Easy to fix in a pressure cooker.

5 bone-in pork chops,
   1/2-inch thick
2 T. oil
14-oz. can Bavarian sauerkraut

5 potatoes, peeled and halved
1/2 c. water
1/4 t. pepper

Heat oil in a 5-quart pressure cooker over high heat. Brown pork chops on both sides, a few at a time; set aside on a plate. Add sauerkraut with juice to drippings in pot; stir to warm through. Layer sauerkraut with pork chops; arrange potatoes on top. Add water and pepper; add water. Close and lock lid. Bring to high pressure; set timer to cook for 15 minutes. Open pressure cooker using natural release method. Arrange on a platter to serve. Makes 5 servings.

Sauerkraut with Caraway

Ginny Watson
Scranton, PA

Delicious with pork roast and potatoes.

2 T. butter
2 slices bacon, chopped
1 c. vegetable broth
3/4 c. water

1/2 c. onion, thinly sliced
3 16-oz. pkgs. refrigerated
   sauerkraut, rinsed
1-1/2 t. caraway seed

Melt butter in a 6-quart electric pressure cooker over medium heat. Cook for 2 minutes, or until slightly browned. Add onion; cook until softened. Stir in remaining ingredients; bring to a boil. Close and lock lid; set heat to high. When cooker comes to high pressure, reduce heat as low as possible. Set timer and cook for 8 minutes. Open pressure cooker using natural release method; let stand 10 minutes. Serves 8.

Meals in an Instant
• ELECTRIC PRESSURE COOKER •

Down-Home Bean Pot

Penny Sherman
Ava, MO

Just plain country cooking, but done quickly in a pressure cooker.

1 c. dried Great Northern, pinto
  or black beans
3 c. chicken broth and/or water
1 T. olive oil
2 thick slices bacon, chopped
1/2 c. onion, chopped
1 stalk celery with leaves,
  chopped
1 carrot, peeled and coarsely
  chopped

1 clove garlic, pressed
1 to 2 sprigs fresh parsley
1 t. dried thyme
1/4 t. pepper
1 dried red chili pepper, rinsed
  and seeded
1/2 bay leaf
salt to taste

Place beans in a deep bowl; add enough water to cover by 2 inches.
Soak for 8 hours or overnight. Drain; rinse and transfer beans to a
5-quart electric pressure cooker. Add remaining ingredients except salt;
stir to combine. Close and lock lid; set heat to high. When pressure
cooker comes to high pressure, turn down heat as low as possible.
Set timer to cook for 10 minutes. Open pressure cooker using natural
release method; let stand for 10 minutes. Open pressure cooker using
natural release method. If too much liquid remains in the pot, simmer
beans for a few minutes, until reduced. Discard chili pepper and bay
leaf; season with salt. Serves 6.

As with slow cookers, electric
pressure cookers should be
filled no more than 2/3 full.
If you're cooking a food that
expands, like dried beans or
pasta, 1/2 full is the limit.

Spiced Orange Pot Roast

Jenita Davison
La Plata, MO

I have been making this roast for over 40 years, but always cooked it on the stovetop until recently, when I purchased an electric pressure cooker. It is so much faster to make now!

1 T. oil
2 to 3-lb. beef chuck roast,
    partially frozen
1/3 c. onion, finely chopped
1/2 t. garlic, minced
11-oz. can mandarin oranges
8-oz. can Spanish-style
    tomato sauce

1 T. sugar
1/4 t. nutmeg
1/4 t. cinnamon
1/8 t. ground cloves
1/8 t. orange zest
1/2 t. salt
pepper to taste
2 T. cornstarch

Add oil to a 6-quart electric pressure cooker; heat over medium-high heat. Brown roast on all sides; remove to a plate. Add onion and garlic to drippings in pot; cook until onion is softened. Return roast to pressure cooker. In a bowl, combine oranges with juice and remaining ingredients except cornstarch; spoon over roast. Close and lock lid. Cook on low pressure for 20 minutes; turn to high pressure and continue cooking for 25 minutes. Transfer roast to a platter; cover with foil and set aside for 10 minutes. To thicken sauce, combine cornstarch and 2 tablespoons of hot cooking liquid; stir back into liquid in pressure cooker. Turn to sauté; simmer for one to 2 minutes, until thickened. Slice roast; serve with sauce. Serves 6.

There's no thawing needed when using frozen ingredients in a pressure cooker. Just add one to 3 minutes to the cooktime.

Meals in an Instant
• ELECTRIC PRESSURE COOKER •

Pot Roast Supper

Julie Dobson
Richmond Hill, GA

*A super-easy recipe when you want a hearty hot meal
for the family without a lot of effort.*

3 to 4-lb. beef chuck roast
14-1/2 oz. can Mexican-style
   diced tomatoes
1 lb. baby carrots
1 c. onion, diced

10-3/4 oz. can cream of
   celery soup
1.35-oz. pkg. onion soup mix
1 T. cornstarch
1/2 c. cold water

Place roast in a 6-quart electric pressure cooker. Add tomatoes with juice, carrots, onion, soup and soup mix. Close and lock lid. Cook on high pressure for 45 minutes. Open pressure cooker using natural release. Transfer roast to a platter; cover with aluminum foil and set aside for 10 minutes. Combine cornstarch and cold water; stir into vegetable mixture in pot. Simmer on sauté until thickened, one to 2 minutes. Slice roast; serve with vegetables and gravy. Makes 8 to 10 servings.

The best cut of beef for a pressure-cooked pot roast is a chuck roast marbled well with fat. The fat will melt while cooking, adding delicious flavor and texture. It's fine to trim away any unusually large pockets of fat.

Herbed Fish Fillets in Packets

Beth Kramer
Port Saint Lucie, FL

My family & friends think I'm a kitchen magician when I whip up these parchment-wrapped packets! The packets can be put together up to 3 hours ahead of time, refrigerated and cooked just before dinnertime. To round out the meal, divide 2 cups of thinly sliced mushrooms and zucchini among the packets.

4 4 to 6-oz. skinless cod,
   halibut or salmon fillets,
   3/4 to 1-inch thick
4 T. olive oil
8 sprigs fresh basil, thyme or
   dill weed
4 green onions, chopped

4 T. butter, diced and divided
1 lemon, cut into 12 thin slices
1/4 c. lemon juice
1/4 c. white wine or chicken
   broth
2 c. water

Tear off 4 squares of parchment paper, each 13 inches long. For each packet, fold a square in half and open again; spray lower half of parchment with non-stick olive oil spray. Place a fish fillet 3 inches from the bottom; brush with one tablespoon oil. Top with 2 herb sprigs, 1/4 of onions, one tablespoon butter and 3 lemon slices. In a small bowl, combine lemon juice and wine or broth. Drizzle 2 tablespoons of juice mixture over fish. Fold down top half of parchment down to meet the bottom edge. Starting on one side, fold and crimp edges to form a tightly sealed, crescent-shaped package. Twist the pointed end around once; fold it underneath. Place a rack or basket in a 5-quart electric pressure cooker; add water. Stack fish packets in a criss-cross heap. Close and lock lid. Set heat to high; bring to high pressure. Reduce heat as low as possible while still on high pressure. Set timer and cook for 5 minutes. Open pressure cooker using quick release method. Lift out packets, one at a time, holding one end with tongs and lifting with a spatula. To serve, place each packet on a dinner plate; cut open with kitchen scissors. Spoon juices in packets over fish; serve immediately. Serves 4.

4-Cheese Macaroni & Cheese

Cheryl Culver
Coyle, OK

Macaroni & cheese is always a favorite, and now it's even faster to make. Rich good flavor with lots of cheese...it always turns out scrumptious! Add some tuna and peas, and you've got Tuna Mac. We love topping it with bacon bits!

4 c. water
16-oz. pkg. elbow macaroni,
    uncooked
2 T. butter, sliced
2 t. salt
12-oz. can evaporated milk

1 t. dry mustard
1 c. mild Cheddar cheese,
    shredded
1/2 c. Swiss cheese, shredded
1/2 c. Gouda cheese, shredded
1/2 c. Havarti cheese, shredded

In a 6-quart electric pressure cooker, combine water, uncooked macaroni, butter and salt; stir gently. Set to high pressure; cook for 2 minutes. Open pressure cooker using 2-minute natural release method. This allows macaroni to continue cooking while any foam that built up inside the pot settles. Once 2-minute natural release has completed, do a slow and controlled pressure release. Open; stir in evaporated milk and mustard. Add cheeses; stir until melted and serve. Makes 8 to 10 servings.

Prefer to shred your own cheese? Place the wrapped block of cheese in the freezer for 15 minutes...it will just glide across the grater! Two cups shredded cheese equals an 8-ounce package.

Coconut Chicken Curry

Jennie Hempfling
Columbus, OH

This goes very well with fragrant basmati rice. I usually cook the rice first, put it in a bowl and cover it while I cook the chicken. If you don't have all the spices, substitute some curry powder along with the salt and pepper.

2 T. olive oil
1 onion, diced
5 t. garlic, minced
1 t. fresh ginger, peeled
   and minced
1-1/2 lbs. boneless, skinless
   chicken thighs, cut into
   quarters, or chicken breasts,
   cut into into 2-inch cubes
1 t. paprika
1 t. turmeric
1 t. ground coriander

1 t. garam masala
1/4 t. cayenne pepper
1/4 t. ground cumin
1 t. salt
1/4 t. pepper
15-oz. can tomato sauce
2 green peppers, coarsely
   chopped
1/2 c. coconut milk
cooked rice
Garnish: chopped fresh parsley
   or cilantro

Press the sauté button on a 5-quart electric pressure cooker; add oil and onion. Cook for 5 to 6 minutes, until tender and translucent. Stir in garlic, ginger, chicken, spices, salt and pepper; cook for one to 2 minutes, until fragrant. Stir in tomato sauce. Close and lock lid; cook on manual high pressure for 8 minutes. Open pressure cooker using quick release method. Press the sauté button and add green peppers; simmer to desired tenderness. Stir in coconut milk. Serve over cooked rice; garnish as desired. Makes 4 servings.

Indian-style naan bread is traditional with curry dishes.
If you can't find any, pita pockets are a good substitute.

Meals in an Instant
• ELECTRIC PRESSURE COOKER •

Honey Bourbon Chicken

Jenita Davison
La Plata, MO

You'll love this delicious, saucy chicken...it tastes just like that chicken you get at the mall. Being able to cook a meal when the meat is frozen is so convenient on busy nights!

4 chicken thighs
1/2 c. onion, diced
1/2 c. honey
1/3 c. soy sauce
1/4 c. catsup
2 T. oil

2 t. garlic, minced
1/4 t. red pepper flakes
1/8 t. pepper
2 T. cornstarch
2 T. water
cooked rice

Arrange chicken thighs in a 5-quart electric pressure cooker. In a bowl, combine remaining ingredients except cornstarch, water and rice; spoon over chicken. Close and lock lid. Set to cook on high pressure for 15 minutes, or 25 minutes if chicken is frozen. Open pressure cooker using natural release method for 5 minutes, then quick release. Transfer chicken to a platter; cover to keep warm. Mix together cornstarch and cold water in a cup. Add to liquid in pressure cooker; cook on sear or sauté until thickened. Serve chicken over cooked rice, topped with sauce from pressure cooker. Serves 4.

For an appetizer that's sure to be a hit, cut Honey Bourbon Chicken into cubes and serve with party picks.

Kale with Garlic & Lemon

Stella Hickman
Gooseberry Patch

This is an easy way to enjoy flavorful, nutritious garden greens.
Try it with collard greens, spinach, Swiss chard or a mix.

1 T. olive oil
3 cloves garlic, slivered
1 lb. fresh kale, stems trimmed
1/2 c. water

1/2 t. salt
juice of 1/2 lemon
pepper to taste

Press the sauté button on an electric pressure cooker; add oil and garlic.
Cook for about 2 minutes, just until garlic is fragrant. Stir in a large
handful of kale; pack in remaining kale. Drizzle water over kale; season
with salt. Close and lock lid; bring up to high pressure using manual
setting. Cook on high pressure for 5 minutes. Open pressure cooker
using quick release method. Drizzle lemon juice over kale; season with
pepper. Serve with a slotted spoon, draining as much liquid as possible.
Serves 4 to 6.

A clean sealing ring ensures fresh, tasty flavors from an electric
pressure cooker. It's easily removed for washing in warm soapy
water, or even in the dishwasher. If any cracks develop in
the sealing ring, it's time to replace it.

Italian Sausages with Onions & Peppers

Mia Rossi
Charlotte, NC

A family favorite! We like to buy homemade Italian sausages with fennel seeds for this from a local Italian grocery. I like to mix & match green, red and yellow peppers for variety and color.

8 sweet or hot Italian pork
   sausage links
2 T. olive oil
3 cloves garlic, minced
2 sweet onions, halved
   and sliced

4 green peppers, sliced
1/4 c. white wine or water
1-1/2 t. Italian seasoning
2/3 c. chicken broth
8 hard rolls, split, or cooked
   polenta

Pierce sausages all over with a knife tip; set aside. In a 6-quart electric pressure cooker, heat oil over medium-high heat until very hot. Working in batches, brown sausages on all sides, about 2 minutes per batch. Transfer sausages to a plate. Add garlic to drippings; cook for 30 seconds. Transfer garlic to plate with a slotted spoon. Add onions and cook until soft; transfer to plate. Add green peppers and cook until soft. Return onions and garlic to pot; toss with peppers. Add wine or water and seasoning; scrape up any browned bits from bottom of pot. Simmer until liquid is completely evaporated. Return sausages and any juices from plate to pot; spoon onion mixture over sausages. Pour broth over all. Close and lock lid. Set heat to high; at high pressure, reduce heat as low as possible. Set timer and cook for 6 minutes. Open pressure cooker using quick release method. Make sure sausages are cooked through; if still pink inside, simmer for several minutes. Serve sausages and onion mixture in hard rolls, or over polenta. Makes 8 servings.

He who enjoys good health is rich, though he knows it not.
– Italian Proverb

Shredded Beef Barbacoa

Stephanie Eakins
Columbus, OH

This deliciously seasoned beef makes a great filling for tacos, burritos, quesadillas, enchilada casseroles or burrito bowls. It can also be frozen for later usage. For a low-carb meal, I like to serve it over shredded red cabbage and lettuce, topped with salsa, sour cream, diced avocado and shredded cheese. So simple...so tasty!

1 T. oil	2 T. chili powder
1 onion, chopped	1 T. brown sugar, packed
1 jalapeño pepper, chopped	2 t. garlic, minced
7-oz. can chipotle salsa	2 t. ground cumin
1/2 c. tomato sauce	1 t. onion powder
1/2 c. beef broth	2 to 3-lb. beef chuck roast
juice of 1 lime	

Press the sauté button on a 6-quart electric pressure cooker; add oil, onion and jalapeño pepper. Cook for 5 to 6 minutes, until tender and translucent. Stir in remaining ingredients except roast. Add roast; turn to coat with sauce. Close and lock lid. Cook on manual high pressure for 60 minutes. Open pressure cooker using natural release method for 20 minutes. Shred roast in pot with 2 forks; serve as desired. Makes 4 to 6 servings.

Treat yourself to a pair of new silicone kitchen gloves. They'll protect your hands from heat (and cold!) for so many tasks, you'll want to use them everyday. They come in lots of fun colors, so choose your favorite!

Meals in an Instant
• ELECTRIC PRESSURE COOKER •

Pressure-Cooker Pulled Pork

Amanda Johnson
Marysville, OH

I whipped this up one evening when I had a couple of extra mouths to feed. It turned out far better than I expected! I served the pork in taco shells, topped with salsa. It would be excellent served in buns with barbecue sauce as well.

8 bone-in pork chops,
    1/2-inch thick
1/4 to 1/2 c. favorite dry
    barbecue seasoning

2 bay leaves
3 c. water
1 onion, quartered
2 cubes beef bouillon

Place a rack or trivet in the bottom of a 6-quart electric pressure cooker. Coat pork chops generously with barbecue seasoning; arrange on rack. Place bay leaves on top; add water, onion and bouillon cubes. Close and lock lid; bring to full pressure on high heat. Reduce heat to medium-high; continue cooking for 30 minutes. Open pressure cooker using natural release method. Transfer pork chops to a cutting board; pull apart with 2 forks. Discard bay leaves; serve as desired. Makes 6 servings.

While the pulled pork is cooking, whip up some delicious sweet potato fries. Slice sweet potatoes into strips or wedges, toss with olive oil and place on a baking sheet. Bake at 400 degrees for 20 to 30 minutes, until tender, turning once. Sprinkle with a little cinnamon-sugar, if you like.

Shredded Chicken Soft Tacos

Chad Rutan
Gooseberry Patch

This savory chicken is delicious not only for stuffing tacos, but serving in burritos, enchiladas and tostadas as well. I like to serve it with Mexican rice and a fresh fruit salad.

2 T. olive oil
1 c. onion, chopped
4 cloves garlic, minced
1 T. chili powder
1/2 c. chicken broth
Optional: 1/3 c. fresh cilantro, chopped
6 boneless, skinless chicken breasts

juice of 3 limes
1-1/2 t. salt
1 t. pepper
12 taco-size flour tortillas, warmed
Garnish: shredded lettuce, diced tomatoes, sliced avocado, shredded Cheddar Jack cheese
Optional: sour cream, salsa

In a 6-quart electric pressure cooker, heat oil over medium-high heat until very hot. Add onion; cook about 3 minutes. Add garlic and chili powder; cook and stir for minute. Add broth; scrape up any browned bits from bottom of pot. Stir in cilantro, if using. Nestle chicken breasts into onion mixture; spoon some of the mixture over them. Drizzle with lime juice; season with salt and pepper. Close and lock lid. Set to high heat; when high pressure is reached, turn down as low as possible while still on high pressure. Set timer and cook for 6 minutes. Open pressure cooker using natural release method; let stand for 15 minutes. Transfer chicken to a cutting board and cool; shred or dice chicken. Transfer contents of pot into a bowl and add chicken; toss to combine. Chicken may be served immediately, or covered and refrigerated up to 3 days. Spoon chicken into tortillas; add toppings as desired. Serves 6, 2 tacos each.

Serve Mexican-style sandwiches for a tasty change. Called tortas, they're hollowed-out crusty bread rolls stuffed with shredded chicken or pork and cheese. Serve cold or toast like a panini sandwich...yum!

Meals in an Instant
• ELECTRIC PRESSURE COOKER •

Grandpa's Pork Tacos

Joni Bitting
Papillion, NE

Whenever Grandpa came to visit, he would make these tacos for the family, and they were everyone's favorite. The pork makes good burritos too. I prefer to brown the roast in a skillet because it's quicker, but you can brown it in your pressure cooker instead.

2 T. olive oil
4-lb. pork shoulder roast
3/4 c. onion, chopped
1 T. garlic, minced
10-oz. can diced tomatoes
    with green chiles
1/2 c. chicken broth
1 T. chili powder

2 T. ground cumin
1 t. Spanish paprika
salt and pepper to taste
20 corn taco shells
Garnish: sour cream, sliced
    avocado, diced tomatoes,
    fresh cilantro

Add oil to a skillet over medium heat; brown roast on both sides, 3 to 4 minutes. Remove roast to a 6-quart electric pressure cooker; set aside. Sauté onion and garlic in skillet for 3 minutes; add to pot. Add tomatoes with juice, broth and spices to pot. Close and lock lid. Cook on high heat for 45 minutes. Open pressure cooker using quick release method. Shred pork with 2 forks, right in the pot. Season with salt and pepper. Serve pork in taco shells, garnished as desired. Makes 10 servings, 2 tacos each.

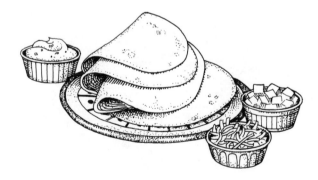

Do you have lots of kids coming over for an after-game party?
Make it easy with do-it-yourself tacos...guests can add their
own favorite toppings. Round out the menu with pitchers
of soft drinks and a yummy dessert. Simple and fun!

71

Big Game Sloppy Joes

Laura Fuller
Fort Wayne, IN

*Popular at all our football get-togethers! If you prefer,
use ground turkey, or a mix of beef and turkey.*

2 T. olive oil
1 c. onion, coarsely chopped
1 red or yellow pepper,
  coarsely chopped
1-1/2 lbs. ground beef or turkey
2 to 3 cloves garlic, chopped
2 T. chili powder
1/2 t. dry mustard
1 t. salt

1/2 t. pepper
12-oz. bottle regular or
  non-alcoholic beer
6-oz. can tomato paste
3 T. light brown sugar, packed
1 T. Worcestershire sauce
6 hamburger buns, split and
  toasted

Press the sauté button on a 5-quart electric pressure cooker. Add oil, onion and red or yellow pepper; cook for about 2 minutes, until softened. Add beef or turkey and garlic. Cook, stirring occasionally, until no longer pink; drain. Stir in seasonings; cook for one to 2 minutes. Add remaining ingredients except buns; stir well. Close and lock the lid. Set heat to high; turn as low as possible once high pressure is reached. Set timer and cook for 5 minutes. Open pressure cooker using quick release method. Serve beef mixture spooned onto buns. Serves 6.

Toast sandwich buns before spooning in Sloppy Joe filling or saucy pulled pork. It only takes a minute and makes such a tasty difference. Buns will drip less too...less mess!

Italian Meatball Sliders

Darrell Lawry
Kissimmee, FL

Get the party going with these yummy mini sandwiches, or super-size it by putting the meatballs on sub rolls with melted cheese on top, drenched in sauce with coleslaw on the side.

2 16-oz. pkgs. frozen meatballs, divided
2 24-oz. jars marinara sauce, divided
14-1/2 oz. can chicken broth
2 T. balsamic vinegar
24 slider rolls, split in half and warmed
6 to 12 slices mozzarella cheese, cut into quarters
24 fresh basil leaves

Coat a 5-quart electric pressure cooker with non-stick olive oil spray. Add one package of frozen meatballs; pour in one jar of sauce. Repeat with remaining meatballs and sauce. Add broth and vinegar; stir gently to coat meatballs. Close and lock the lid. Cook on high heat for 18 minutes, turning heat as low as possible once high pressure is reached. Open pressure cooker using quick release method. Stir gently; let stand for 5 to 10 minutes. To serve, fill each each roll with 2 meatballs, a spoonful of sauce, one or 2 pieces of cheese and a basil leaf. Fasten with a party pick, if desired. Makes 12 servings, 2 sliders each.

Wondering what to do with the rest of the bottle of balsamic vinegar? Add a dash to tomato sauces, or mix up a vinaigrette dressing. You can even cook it down to make a flavorful drizzle for steamed veggies.

Homemade Meatballs

Kay Marone
Des Moines, IA

*My sons love these meatballs! They're ready in a jiffy
to serve over spaghetti or as meatball sandwiches.*

2 T. olive oil
1 T. garlic, minced
2 lbs. ground beef
1 c. grated Parmesan cheese
1/2 c. milk

3/4 c. Italian-flavored dry
   bread crumbs
28-oz. can tomato purée
1-1/2 c. water
Optional: shredded cheese

Press the sauté button on a 5-quart electric pressure cooker; add oil and garlic. In a large bowl, combine beef, cheese, milk and bread crumbs; mix well and form into golf ball-size meatballs. Add meatballs to cooker as they are formed; brown lightly. Stir in tomato purée and water. Close lid and lock. Press meat button and set timer to cook for for 6 minutes. Open pressure cooker using natural release method. Sprinkle with cheese, if desired. Makes 4 to 6 servings.

Finger-Lickin' Ribs

Tori Willis
Champaign, IL

Serve as an appetizer...simply cut into single ribs after cooking.

3-lb. rack pork baby back ribs
salt and pepper to taste

1 c. water
1/2 c. favorite barbecue sauce

Cut ribs into serving-size pieces; season generously with salt and pepper. Place a rack or trivet in a 6-quart electric pressure cooker; add water. Arrange ribs on rack. Close and lock lid lid. Cook on high pressure for 20 minutes (tender) or 25 minutes (falling off the bone). Open pressure cooker using natural release method. Transfer ribs to a baking sheet; brush with sauce. Bake at 450 degrees for 10 to 15 minutes. Makes 4 to 6 servings.

Meals in an Instant
• ELECTRIC PRESSURE COOKER •

Chinese Soy Chicken Wings

Zoe Bennett
Columbia, SC

*My family loves these spicy, sticky wings. Serve with steamed rice
and a steamed veggie for dinner, or let them steal the show
at your next party. Pass the napkins, please!*

1/3 c. chicken broth
1/3 c. sherry or chicken broth
1/3 c. soy sauce
2 t. fresh ginger, peeled and
   grated
2 t. Dijon mustard

1 clove garlic, pressed
1/4 t. red pepper flakes
24 chicken wings, separated
1/4 c. apricot jam
1 T. cornstarch
1 T. cold water

In a large container, combine all ingredients except chicken wings, jam,
cornstarch and water. Add wings to bowl; toss to coat evenly. Cover
and refrigerate for 2 hours to overnight, stirring twice. Transfer wings to
a 6-quart electric pressure cooker. Pour marinade into a small saucepan;
bring to a boil and pour over wings. Close and lock lid; set heat to high.
When pressure cooker reaches high pressure, turn down heat as low as
possible. Set timer and cook for 14 minutes; turn off. Let stand for
5 minutes. Open pressure cooker using quick release method. Transfer
wings to a platter; set aside. Stir jam into liquid in pot; whisk until
melted. Stir together cornstarch and cold water in a cup; add to pot
and stir well. Return wings to pot; stir gently to coat evenly. Simmer
for 2 minutes, or until sauce is thickened and translucent. Transfer
wings to a serving plate, using tongs. Makes about 2 dozen.

Peel fresh ginger with a spoon rather than a knife.
It's faster and safer, plus less will go to waste too!

Cheesy Southwest Corn & Bacon Dip

Rhonda Reeder
Ellicott City, MD

My whole family loves this cheesy, corny dip. My teenage sons would take the whole pot to their room and eat it all themselves, if they could get away with it!

1 T. olive oil
4 to 6 slices bacon, chopped
1-1/2 c. frozen corn
1/4 c. onion, diced
1 jalapeño pepper, chopped and
    seeds removed
1 clove garlic, minced
14-1/2 oz. can diced tomatoes
4-oz. can diced green chiles

8-oz. pkg. cream cheese,
    softened and cubed
2 t. chili powder
1 t. ground cumin
1/2 t. salt
1 c. shredded Cheddar or
    Pepper Jack cheese
scoop-type corn or tortilla chips

Select the sauté function on a 4-quart electric pressure cooker; drizzle with oil. Add bacon; cook to desired crispness. Remove bacon to a paper towel, reserving drippings in pot. Add corn, onion and jalapeño; cook for 4 to 5 minutes. Stir in garlic; add tomatoes with juice, chiles, cream cheese and seasonings. Close and lock lid. Cook on manual high pressure for 5 minutes. Open pressure cooker using quick release method. Add bacon and shredded cheese; stir until cheese is melted. If necessary, select sauté again and cook until hot and bubbly. Serve warm with corn or tortilla chips. Serves 8.

Serve up homemade lemonade... it couldn't be simpler! In a large saucepan, combine 2 quarts water and 1/2 cup sugar. Heat just until the sugar dissolves. Remove from heat and pour in 3/4 cup lemon juice. Mix well and chill.

Spinach-Artichoke Dip

Lynn Williams
Muncie, IN

*This has been my family's favorite dip for get-togethers for decades!
Mom used to make it in the oven, then my sister found a slow-cooker
recipe. Now I'm making it in my new pressure cooker. It's easier than
ever and just as yummy! Serve with tortilla chips or your favorite
snacking crackers.*

1 c. water
14-oz. can artichoke hearts,
    drained and chopped
10-oz. pkg. frozen chopped
    spinach, thawed
8-oz. pkg. cream cheese, cubed
1/2 c. plain Greek yogurt

1 c. shredded mozzarella cheese
1/2 c. grated Parmesan cheese
 1/2 c. onion, finely chopped
2 cloves garlic, minced
1 t. Worcestershire sauce
salt and pepper to taste

Pour water into a 6-quart electric pressure cooker; place a rack or trivet
in pot and set aside. Spray a 2-quart casserole dish with non-stick
vegetable spray. Press as much liquid as possible out of artichokes and
spinach; add to dish. Add remaining ingredients to dish; blend well and
set on rack. Close and lock lid. Select high pressure; set timer and cook
for 10 minutes. Open pressure cooker using natural release method.
Remove dish; stir again and serve warm. Serves 6.

Bring along a tasty appetizer to the next gathering! Tuck a
loaf of pumpernickel bread filled with a delicious hot dip
into a basket, surround with bread cubes and deliver
to your hostess...she'll love it!

Lemon Bread Pudding

Marian Buckley
Fontana, CA

I have a lemon tree in my backyard, and I'm always looking for new ways to use them. This recipe was a hit...tart, lemony goodness in a bread pudding. I like to serve it warm, drizzled with cream.

3 to 3-1/2 c. day-old
  French bread, cut into
  1/2-inch cubes
1-1/2 T. lemon zest
1 c. whipping cream
1 c. whole milk
4 eggs, divided
3/4 c. sugar

3 T. butter, melted and slightly
  cooled
1/8 t. salt
1/2 c. lemon juice
2 c. water
Garnish: powdered sugar,
  fresh berries
Optional: fresh mint sprigs

Spray a 2-quart casserole dish with non-stick butter-flavored spray. Combine bread cubes and lemon zest in dish; toss to mix and set aside. In a bowl, whisk together cream, milk, 3 beaten eggs, sugar, melted butter and salt; set aside. In a small bowl, beat together remaining egg, salt and lemon juice. Add to cream mixture and beat well. Pour cream mixture over bread cubes; press down to make sure bread is soaked. Let stand 10 minutes. Cover dish with aluminum foil; loosely tuck ends underneath. Place a rack or trivet in a 6-quart electric pressure cooker; add water. Criss-cross 2 long strips of aluminum foil for handles; set dish on the rack. Close and lock lid. Set heat to high; reduce heat as low as possible once high pressure is reached. Set timer and cook for 20 minutes. Open pressure cooker using natural release method; let stand for 15 minutes. Remove dish, using the foil handles to carefully lift it out. Set on a wire rack; loosen foil. Pudding should test clean with a toothpick. Serve warm; garnish as desired. Makes 4 servings.

Meals in an Instant
• ELECTRIC PRESSURE COOKER •

Salted Caramel Cheesecake
Kimberlee Eakins
Cleveland, OH

You'll love this creamy cheesecake! The flaked salt is optional, but I really like the salty-sweet taste.

2 8-oz. pkgs. cream cheese,
   room temperature
1/2 c. light brown sugar, packed
1/4 c. sour cream
1 T. all-purpose flour
1/2 t. salt

1-1/2 t. vanilla extract
2 eggs, beaten
2 c. water
Garnish: 1/2 c. caramel topping
Optional: 1 t. flaked sea salt

Make Buttery Cracker Crust; set aside. In a bowl, beat cream cheese and brown sugar with an electric mixer on medium speed until blended. Add sour cream; beat for 30 more seconds. Beat in flour, salt and vanilla. Add eggs; beat until just smooth. Pour mixture into crust; set aside. Set pan on a paper towel; place a length of foil underneath. Wrap foil over bottom of pan. Fold a long piece of foil in half lengthwise; center pan on foil. Pour water into a 6-quart electric pressure cooker; add a rack or trivet. Using the foil as handles, place pan into pot. Close and lock lid. Set to manual high pressure; set timer to 35 minutes. Open using natural release method. Remove pan from pot using foil handles; set on a wire rack and cool for one hour. Cover cheesecake in pan with foil; refrigerate at least 4 hours or overnight. At serving time, loosen sides of the cheesecake from the pan with a table knife, release sides of the pan. Cut into wedges; garnish as desired. Serves 6.

Buttery Cracker Crust:

1-1/2 c. buttery round crackers,
   finely crushed

1/4 c. butter, melted
2 T. sugar

Spray a 7" springform pan lightly with non-stick vegetable spray. Line with a 7-inch circle of parchment paper; spray again and set aside. Combine all ingredients; mix well. Press mixture firmly into bottom and up sides of pan.

Easy Cherry Dump Cake

Ann Tober
Biscoe, AR

This dessert is so good and so simple. At first, everyone says, "There's no way that was made in a pressure cooker!" But it is, and it's as easy as can be. Delicious with apple pie filling too.

2 c. white or yellow cake mix
3 T. butter, melted
21-oz. can cherry pie filling

2 c. water
Garnish: vanilla ice cream

Pour dry cake mix into a bowl; add melted butter. Stir until combined; mixture will be a bit lumpy. Add pie filling; mix until combined. Pour batter into a lightly greased 7" round cake pan or casserole dish; cover top of pan with aluminum foil. Pour water into a 6-quart electric pressure cooker. Add a rack or trivet; set pan on rack. Close and lock lid. Set to manual high pressure for 25 minutes. Open pressure cooker using natural release method. Let stand for 5 to 10 minutes. Scoop out cake; serve topped with a scoop of ice cream. Makes 10 to 12 servings.

A 7-inch springform pan is perfect for a 6-quart electric pressure cooker...just be sure to cover the bottom with foil to prevent leaks. A a round cake pan or oven-safe round glass casserole dish works well too...just check first to make sure it fits!

Meals in an Instant
• ELECTRIC PRESSURE COOKER •

Maple-Pumpkin Custard Cups
Lynda Robson
Boston, MA

*Your Thanksgiving guests will be impressed by this creamy
pumpkin custard in its own little cups! Make them a day
ahead and chill, then just pull from the fridge to serve.*

1-1/2 c. whole milk,
   or 1 c. whole milk plus
   1/2 c. whipping cream
4 eggs, beaten
3/4 c. canned pumpkin
2/3 c. pure maple syrup

1/2 t. cinnamon
1/2 t. nutmeg
1/4 t. salt
2 c. water
Garnish: whipped cream,
   nutmeg

In a microwave-safe glass measuring cup, microwave milk just until
steaming; allow to cool slightly. In a bowl, whisk together eggs,
pumpkin and maple syrup until smooth. Slowly add milk to egg
mixture, whisking constantly. Stir in spices and salt. Pour into 6 lightly
greased 6-ounce custard cups. Cover each cup tightly with aluminum
foil. Place a steamer basket in a 5-quart electric pressure cooker; add
water. Arrange 3 custard cups in basket. Set a rack on top; arrange
remaining cups on top. (It's fine if cups are touching.) Close and lock
lid; set heat to high and bring to high pressure. Turn heat as low as
possible while still on high pressure. Set timer and cook for 10 minutes.
Open pressure cooker using natural release method; let stand for
15 minutes. Using tongs, remove custard cups to a wire rack. Let cool
at room temperature for about one hour. Cover cups with plastic wrap;
refrigerate for 4 hours to overnight before serving. Garnish with a dollop
of whipped cream and a sprinkle of nutmeg. Makes 6 servings.

For a delicious non-dairy Coconut-
Pumpkin Custard, replace the milk
with unsweetened coconut milk.
Use sugar instead of maple syrup
and add 1/2 teaspoon coconut
extract. Garnish with toasted
coconut. Yum!

Maple Apple Crisp

Linda Peterson
Mason, MI

*My family loves this dessert! This is the only way
I will make it from now on.*

5 cooking apples, peeled,
  cored and chopped
2 t. cinnamon
1/2 t. nutmeg
1/2 c. water
1 T. pure maple syrup

1/4 c. butter, melted
3/4 c. rolled oats, uncooked
1/4 c. all-purpose flour
1/4 c. brown sugar, packed
1/2 t. salt
Optional: vanilla ice cream

Add apples to a 5-quart electric pressure cooker; sprinkle with spices.
Drizzle with water and maple syrup; toss to mix and set aside. In a
bowl, mix together remaining ingredients except water and garnish.
Drop batter over apples by spoonfuls. Close and lock lid. Use manual
setting to cook on high pressure for 8 minutes. Open pressure cooker
using natural release method; let stand for several minutes. Sauce will
thicken. Serve warm, topped with ice cream if desired. Makes 3 to
4 servings.

Warm caramel ice cream topping makes a delightful drizzle
over Maple Apple Crisp. Just heat it in the microwave for
a few seconds, and it's ready to spoon over desserts.

Slowly Simmered Flavors

Cheesy Ham & Potatoes

Sharon Nunn
Mechanicsville, VA

*This recipe was shared by a friend, and I tweaked it to my family's
taste. My boys request it often. It's good for breakfast or dinner...
really, any time of day. Creamy, dreamy comfort to serve with a smile!*

30-oz. pkg. frozen shredded
   hashbrowns
1 c. cooked ham, cubed
8-oz. pkg. shredded sharp
   Cheddar cheese, divided

10-3/4 oz. can cream of
   chicken soup
12-oz. can evaporated milk
1 t. salt
1/2 t. pepper

Place frozen hashbrowns in a 4-quart slow cooker. Add ham and
1-1/2 cups cheese; stir well and set aside. In a bowl, whisk together
soup, milk and seasonings; add to hashbrown mixture and stir until
combined. Cover and cook on low setting for 4 to 5 hours. Top
with remaining cheese; cover and let stand until cheese is melted.
Makes 8 servings.

A cool fruit salad is perfect with a warm slow-cooker
brunch dish...easy to make ahead of time too. Toss together
ripe fruits like blueberries, strawberries and kiwi fruit.
Drizzle with a dressing made by whisking together 1/2 cup
honey, 1/4 cup lime juice and one teaspoon lime zest.

Slowly Simmered Flavors
• SLOW COOKER •

Cherry-Almond Oatmeal

Sandy Churchill
West Bridgewater, MA

This is one of our family's favorite cool-weather breakfasts. Enjoy the comforts of home and wake up to the cozy scent of cherry pie! I usually make this at the start of a busy week, so we can enjoy the leftovers throughout the week.

1 c. steel-cut oats, uncooked
1 c. quick-cooking oats,
    uncooked
20-oz. can cherry pie filling
1/2 t. almond extract

2 c. water
1 t. cinnamon
2 T. brown sugar, packed
Optional: milk

Add all ingredients except optional milk to a 4-quart slow cookers; stir well. Cover and cook on low setting for 8 hours, or overnight. Serve topped with milk, if desired. Serves 8 to 10.

Add a splash of color to the breakfast table...it wakes everyone up! Mix & match cheery plates, set out spunky retro juice glasses and arrange sunny marigolds and red-hot zinnias together in a vase.

Danny's Brown Sugar Oatmeal

Pam Littel
Pleasant View, TN

My son loves this comforting breakfast dish and will often fix it for the family.

4 c. milk
2 c. quick-cooking oats, uncooked
2 c. apples, peeled, cored and diced

1 c. raisins
1/2 c. brown sugar, packed
1/4 c. pure maple syrup
2 T. butter, melted
2 t. cinnamon

Spray a 5-quart slow cooker with non-stick spray. Combine all ingredients in slow cooker. Cover and cook on low setting for 6 hours. Stir before serving. Makes 6 servings.

Store brown sugar in an airtight container to keep it soft. If it's already turned hard, place brown sugar in a microwave-safe bowl and cover first with a damp paper towel, then plastic wrap. Microwave on high for 30 seconds to one minute, fluff with a fork and use immediately.

Slowly Simmered Flavors
• SLOW COOKER •

Gooey Cinnamon Rolls

Laura Fuller
Fort Wayne, IN

These go together in a jiffy! Then on Saturdays, when my sisters and I get back from early-morning garage sales, we enjoy these rolls together with some hot coffee.

2 12-oz. tubes cinnamon rolls,
    cut into quarters and divided
4 eggs, beaten
1/2 c. whipping cream
1/4 c. pure maple syrup

2 t. vanilla extract
1 t. cinnamon
1 t. nutmeg
Optional: 1/2 c. chopped pecans

Spray a 4-quart slow cooker with non-stick vegetable spray. Arrange half of cinnamon roll pieces in the bottom of slow cooker; set aside icing packets. In a small bowl, whisk together eggs, cream, maple syrup, vanilla and spices. Spoon over cinnamon rolls in slow cooker. Layer remaining cinnamon roll pieces on top; drizzle one packet of icing over rolls. Cover and cook on low setting for 2 to 2-1/2 hours, until rolls are set and golden at the sides. Remove crock from slow cooker. Drizzle remaining icing packet over top; sprinkle with nuts, if using. Serve warm. Serves 6 to 8.

Slow cookers are so handy, you may want more than one!
A 5- or 6-quart model is just right for families and potlucks,
while a smaller 3-quart one can be used for dips and sauces.

Rich & Thick Stuffed Green Pepper Soup

Debra Arch
Kewanee, IL

This hearty soup has many layers of delicious flavor and is easy to make. Slow cooking allows all the flavors to simmer and blend together when entertaining. It smells delicious and makes everyone ask, "What's for dinner, and how soon can we eat?"

2 lbs. ground beef
28-oz. can diced tomatoes
28-oz. can tomato sauce
3 c. cocktail vegetable juice
2-1/2 c. green pepper, chopped
1-1/2 c. long-cooking rice,
    uncooked

2 cubes beef bouillon
1/4 c. brown sugar, packed
2 t. salt
1 t. pepper

Brown beef in a large skillet over medium heat; drain. Stir in tomatoes with juice and remaining ingredients; bring to a boil. Transfer to a 6-quart slow cooker. Cover and cook on low setting for 2 hours, or until peppers are tender. Serves 8 to 10.

Stir up a loaf of beer bread to serve with hot soup. Combine
3 cups self-rising flour, a 12-ounce can of beer and
3 tablespoons sugar in a greased loaf pan. Bake for
25 minutes at 350 degrees; drizzle with melted butter.

Slowly Simmered Flavors
• SLOW COOKER •

3-Bean Vegetarian Chili

Stephanie Nicholson
Ontario, Canada

We love chilis, soups and stews on chilly days. But sometimes a more health-conscious option is in order after a long winter of comfort food! So this is our favorite protein-packed dish...and it's so easy to do in the slow cooker!

2 14-1/2 oz. cans diced tomatoes
14-1/2 oz. can crushed tomatoes
15-1/2 oz. can kidney beans,
   drained and rinsed
15-1/2 oz. black beans, drained
   and rinsed
15-1/2 oz. cannellini beans,
   drained and rinsed
1 to 2 carrots, peeled and
   chopped

1 zucchini, chopped
1 onion, chopped
3 cloves garlic, minced
1 T. chili powder
salt and pepper to taste
Optional: 2 T. brown sugar,
   packed
cooked quinoa
Garnish: sour cream, chopped
   green onions

In a 6-quart slow cooker, combine tomatoes with juice and remaining ingredients except quinoa and garnish. Stir well. Cover and cook on low setting for 6 hours, or on high setting for 2-1/2 hours. Serve chili over cooked quinoa; garnish as desired. Makes 6 to 8 servings.

Simple slow-cooker recipes are ideal for older children just learning to cook. With supervision, they can learn to use can openers, paring knives and hot mitts...and they'll be proud to serve the meal they've prepared!

Kathy's 8-Can Taco Soup

Katherine Nelson
Centerville, UT

My friend shared this recipe with me. She has made this for our bunco group a few times, and it is so good. She always serves it with freshly baked rolls...it's the perfect combination! You can use hotter sauce if you want it spicier.

14-1/2 oz. can petite diced
   tomatoes, drained
15-1/2 oz. can black beans,
   drained and rinsed
15-1/2 oz. pinto beans, drained
   and rinsed
15-oz. can corn, drained
14-oz. can chicken broth

12-1/2 oz. can chicken, drained
   and broken up
10-3/4 oz. can cream of
   chicken soup
10-oz. can green enchilada sauce
1-1/4 oz. pkg. taco seasoning
   mix

Combine tomatoes with juice and remaining ingredients in a 6-quart slow cooker. Cover and cook on high setting for 3 to 4 hours, until hot and bubbly. Makes 6 servings.

Ham & White Bean Soup

Amy Butcher
Columbus, GA

So convenient...no soaking needed! We like this with cornbread.

1 lb. dried Great Northern Beans.
   rinsed and sorted
1 lb. cooked ham, cubed
6 to 7 c. chicken broth

2/3 c. onion, diced
1 t. dried oregano
1 t. dried parsley
salt and pepper to taste

Combine all ingredients in a 6-quart slow cooker; stir. Cover and cook on low setting for 8 hours. Makes 8 servings.

For thick, creamy bean soup with no cream added, use a hand-held immersion blender to purée some of the cooked beans right in the slow cooker.

Slowly Simmered Flavors
• SLOW COOKER •

Chicken Posole

Teresa Grimsley
Alamosa, CO

A favorite at our house, especially in fall and winter. With this recipe, it's easy to use up a lot of odds & ends in the fridge too. You can add almost any vegetable, and it always turns out great!

14-1/2 oz. can Mexican-
  seasoned diced tomatoes
16-oz. can black, kidney or
  pinto beans, drained
15-oz. can hominy, drained
10-oz. can green enchilada sauce
  or salsa verde
1 to 2 4-oz. cans sliced black
  olives, drained
4-oz. can diced green chiles

2 to 3 carrots, chopped
2 to 3 stalks celery, chopped
3/4 c. onion, chopped
3 cloves garlic, minced
2 t. ground cumin
1-1/2 lbs. boneless, skinless
  chicken breasts or thighs
Garnish: sour cream, chopped
  fresh cilantro, lime wedges,
  tortilla chips

In a 6-quart slow cooker, combine tomatoes with juice and remaining ingredients except chicken and garnish. Stir well to mix. Place chicken on top. Cover and cook on high setting for 3 to 3-1/2 hours, until vegetables are tender and chicken is done. Remove chicken to a plate; skim any fat from surface. Shred chicken, using 2 forks; return to slow cooker and stir into soup. Just before serving, stir in cilantro. Ladle into bowls; serve with desired garnishes. Serves 8 to 10.

It's a cinch to warm tortillas for your favorite Mexican dish.
Place several tortillas on a microwave-safe plate and
cover with a dampened paper towel. Microwave on high
for 30 seconds to one minute.

Sticks-to-Your-Ribs
Chicken & Wild Rice Soup

Anita Gibson
Woodbury, MN

I struggled to find a thick and delicious yet low-fat wild rice soup that I could make in the morning, then serve when I got home from church. After some experimentation, I came up with this wonderful scrumptious soup made in the slow cooker. I hope you like it too!

32-oz. container chicken broth
2 10-3/4 oz. cans low-sodium
    cream of chicken soup
10-3/4 oz. can low-sodium
    cream of mushroom soup
1 lb. cooked chicken, diced
1 c. wild rice, uncooked

1 c. sliced mushrooms
1/2 c. onion, diced
1/2 c. celery, diced
1/2 c. carrot, peeled and diced
1 clove garlic, minced
1/4 c. light cream or milk

Combine all ingredients except cream or milk in a 6-quart slow cooker. Cover and cook on low setting for 6 to 8 hours; stir in cream or milk during the last 2 hours of cooking. If finished soup is too thick, thin to desired consistency with a little milk or water. Makes 6 servings.

If you enjoy creamy soups, try substituting canned evaporated milk for half-and-half or whole milk. It holds up well in slow-cooker recipes, is easy to keep on hand and is lower in fat too.

Slowly Simmered Flavors
• SLOW COOKER •

Homemade Chicken Stew

Patty Hancock
Hawthorne, NJ

I created this healthy recipe as a light meal my family could enjoy.

2 lbs. boneless, skinless chicken
    breasts, cubed
2 to 3 carrots, peeled and sliced
2 stalks broccoli, cut up
1 yellow squash, sliced
1 zucchini, sliced

1 onion, halved and sliced
2 32-oz. cans low-sodium
    chicken broth
2 c. water
1 T. chicken soup base

Add chicken and vegetables to a 5-quart slow cooker. Pour broth over all; add soup base and water. Cover and cook on low setting for 7 to 8 hours. Serves 8.

Hearty Alfredo Chicken Stew

Jill Ball
Highland, UT

Nothing is better than coming home from a long day of work
to the aroma of a delicious hot dinner, ready to serve!

15-oz. jar Alfredo pasta sauce
3/4 c. water
1/2 t. dried basil
1/2 t. salt
2 15-oz. cans diced potatoes,
    drained

1-1/4 lbs. boneless, skinless
    chicken breasts, cut into
    strips 1-inch wide
16-oz. pkg. frozen mixed
    vegetables

Spray a 4-quart slow cooker with cooking spray. In a small bowl, mix pasta sauce, water and seasonings; set aside. In slow cooker, layer half each of potatoes, chicken strips, frozen vegetables and sauce mixture. Repeat layers. Cover and cook on low setting for 6 to 8 hours. Serves 6.

Keep store-bought frozen, chopped onions on hand... they save chopping time!

Mushroom Beef Stew

Joan White
Malvern, PA

Just imagine coming home on a cold winter night and being greeted by the delicious aroma of a hearty stew, ready to serve!

2 to 3 lbs. stew beef cubes
1/4 c. all-purpose flour
1 t. dried thyme
1 t. salt
1/2 t. pepper
3/4 c. beef broth
1/4 c. red wine or beef broth

1/4 c. tomato paste
3 cloves garlic, minced
3/4 lb. cremini, shiitake or
    button mushrooms, quartered
1 c. baby carrots, halved
Garnish: fresh parsley, chopped

Place beef cubes in a slow cooker; set aside. In a cup, combine flour and seasonings; sprinkle over beef and toss to coat. In a small bowl, combine broth, wine or broth, tomato paste and garlic. Mix well and add to beef in slow cooker. Add mushrooms and carrots; mix well. Cover and cook on low setting for 8 to 9 hours, or on high setting for 5 to 6 hours, until beef and vegetables are tender. Just before serving, stir well; garnish with parsley. Makes 8 servings.

Fluffy dumplings are tasty in hearty soups and stews.
About 30 minutes before soup is done, mix up 2 cups biscuit
baking mix with 3/4 cup milk. Drop by tablespoonfuls onto
simmering soup. Cover and cook on high setting
for 20 to 25 minutes...done!

Slowly Simmered Flavors
• SLOW COOKER •

Beef Barley Soup

Melody Taynor
Everett, WA

*My family just loves this veggie-packed soup. It's perfect for when
I come back from the farmers' market with a basket of fresh produce.*

2 lbs. stew beef cubes
salt and pepper to taste
2 T. oil
10 c. water, divided
3 to 3-1/2 T. beef soup base
2 c. celery, chopped

2 onions, chopped
5 cloves garlic, minced
2 c. potatoes, peeled and diced
2 c. carrots, peeled and diced
1 c. pearl barley, uncooked

Season beef cubes well with salt and pepper; set aside. Heat oil in a
heavy skillet over medium heat. Working in batches, brown beef;
transfer to a 6-quart slow cooker. When beef is browned, add 2 cups
water to same skillet. Stir up browned bits in skillet and bring to a boil;
transfer mixture to slow cooker. Add remaining water, soup base,
celery, onions and garlic to slow cooker; stir. Cover and cook on low
setting for 6 hours. Add potatoes and carrots; cover and cook for
another hour. Add barley; cook for one additional hour, or until barley
is tender. Makes 6 servings.

All-day slow cooking works wonders on less-expensive,
less-tender cuts of beef. Chuck roast, rump roast, round steak
and stew beef all cook up juicy and delicious.

Loaded Baked Potato Soup

Beth Flack
Terre Haute, IN

I like to serve this delicious soup with a loaf of crusty bread on cool fall evenings. Save out a little of the bacon and chives to garnish each bowl, if you like.

1/4 c. butter, sliced
1 onion, finely chopped
2 stalks celery, chopped
1 t. salt
1-1/2 t. pepper
8 russet potatoes, peeled and
    cut into 1/2-inch cubes
1 t. garlic, minced

2 14-oz. cans chicken broth
8-oz. container sour cream
8-oz. container whipping cream
8-oz. pkg. shredded Cheddar
    cheese
20-oz. pkg. real bacon crumbles
1/4 c. fresh chives, chopped

Add butter to a 5-quart slow cooker on high setting. When butter melts, add onion, celery and seasonings. Stir; let cook for several minutes. Add potatoes, garlic and broth. Turn slow cooker to low setting; cover and cook for 7 to 8 hours. Remove 1/4 cup of potatoes to a small bowl and mash; return to slow cooker. Stir in remaining ingredients; cover and cook for one additional hour. Serves 6.

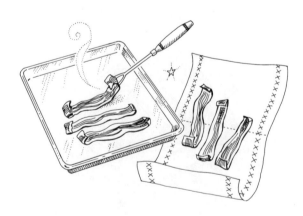

A quick, no-mess way to cook bacon! Arrange slices on a broiler pan and place 3 to 4 inches under the broiler. Broil for one to 2 minutes on each side, depending on how crispy you like your bacon.

Slowly Simmered Flavors
• SLOW COOKER •

Southwest Beef Stew

Tonya Sheppard
Galveston, TX

Serve with your favorite white corn tortilla chips and
a dollop of sour cream.

2 lbs. stew beef cubes
14-1/2 oz. can diced tomatoes
4 c. beef broth

16-oz. jar southwest salsa with
   corn and black beans
15-oz. can hominy, drained

Combine beef, tomatoes with juice and remaining ingredients in a
5-quart slow cooker; stir. Cover and cook on low setting for 8 to
10 hours. Makes 6 servings.

1-2-3 Beef Stew

Kathy Courington
Canton, GA

An easy stew to make when you're on the go. Toss everything
together in the slow cooker, turn it on and you're all set.

3 lbs. stew beef cubes
2 10-3/4 oz. cans cream of
   mushroom soup
3/4 c. water

1.35-oz. pkg. onion soup mix
Optional: cooked rice or egg
   noodles

Combine all ingredients except rice or noodles in a 6-quart slow cooker.
Cover and cook on low setting for 7 to 8 hours. Serve over cooked rice
or noodles, if desired. Makes 6 to 8 servings.

To brown or not to brown? It isn't really necessary with
roasts and stew beef, but adds a lot of flavor. Coat with
all-purpose flour and brown with a little oil in a skillet,
then add to recipe as directed.

2-Pepper White Chicken Chili
Diane Cohen
Breinigsville, PA

*I combined two recipes to come up with this one...
it's become a family favorite!*

1 T. canola oil
1 green pepper, chopped
1 jalapeño pepper, seeded
   and chopped
3/4 c. onion, chopped
1 T. garlic, chopped
2 14-1/2 oz. cans Great Northern
   beans, drained and rinsed
14-oz. can chicken broth

2 lbs. boneless, skinless
   chicken breasts
1 T. plus 1/2 t. ground cumin
1 T. lime juice
Garnish: shredded Cheddar Jack
   cheese
Optional: sour cream, chopped
   fresh cilantro

Heat oil in a large non-stick skillet over medium-high heat. Add
peppers, onion and garlic. Cover and cook, stirring occasionally, for
6 minutes. Transfer pepper mixture to a 4-quart slow cooker; stir in
beans and broth. Add chicken, pushing down into mixture. Add cumin
and lime juice. Cover and cook on low setting for 6 to 7 hours, or on
high setting for 4 hours. Top individual bowls with shredded cheese,
sour cream and cilantro, as desired. Serves 4.

Host a neighborhood chili cook-off. Invite everyone to
bring slow cookers filled with their own special chili...
you provide tasty toppings and warm cornbread on
the side. Be sure to have a prize for the winner!

Slowly Simmered Flavors
• SLOW COOKER •

Grandma's Famous Chili

Krysti Hilfiger
Covington, PA

One day every fall, our family & friends gather to press apple cider the old-fashioned way, and Grandma always serves this chili. It's really perfect for those busy days and so easy to make...why not double the recipe and have dinner for another day?

1 lb. ground beef, browned
   and drained
2 28-oz. cans crushed tomatoes
2 15-1/2 oz. cans kidney beans,
   drained

1 T. chili powder
3 T. dried, chopped onion
salt and pepper to taste
sugar to taste
saltine crackers

Combine all ingredients except saltine crackers in a 5-quart slow cooker; stir. Cover and cook on high setting for 4 to 6 hours. Serve with saltines. Serves 5 to 8.

If you like sweet cornbread, you'll love this! Mix together an 8-1/2 ounce box of corn muffin mix, a 9-ounce box of yellow cake mix, 1/2 cup water, 1/3 cup milk and 2 beaten eggs. Pour into a greased 13"x9" baking pan and bake at 350 degrees for 15 to 20 minutes. Scrumptious!

Oklahoma Rancher Soup

Carol Davis
Edmond, OK

*This soup makes the kitchen smell so good on chilly winter days...
really cheers you up! Serve with buttered cornbread and
a tossed green salad for a wonderful winter meal.*

1 lb. ground beef, browned
   and drained
2-1/2 c. water
1.35-oz. pkg. onion soup mix
1-1/2 t. chili powder
2 14-1/2 oz. cans diced tomatoes

2 carrots, peeled and diced
2 russet potatoes, peeled
   and diced
1 red pepper, chopped
1/2 c. celery, sliced
1/4 c. pearled barley, uncooked

In a 4-quart slow cooker, combine beef, water, soup mix and chili
powder; mix well. Add tomatoes with juice and remaining ingredients.
Cover and cook on low setting for 7 to 8 hours, or high setting for
3-1/2 to 4 hours. Makes 4 to 6 servings.

It's a good idea to test new recipes by staying nearby and
checking the dish now & then...but don't lift the lid too often.
That way, you'll know exactly how long the recipe takes
to cook in your slow cooker. Feel free to make
a note in your cookbook!

Slowly Simmered Flavors
• SLOW COOKER •

Beef-Vegetable Soup

Teresa Niemi
Bonifay, FL

My kids won't eat "real" onions, so I use dried onions
in this recipe and they don't know the difference. Shh!

1 lb. ground beef chuck
1/4 c. dried, minced onion
1/2 t. salt
1/4 t. pepper
14-1/2 oz. can Italian-seasoned
   diced tomatoes
3 to 4 potatoes, peeled and cubed

3 c. water
1-1/2 c. vegetable cocktail juice
1 c. carrots, peeled and sliced
2 T. sugar or sugar substitute
1 t. dried parsley
1 t. dried basil
1 bay leaf

In a non-stick skillet, cook beef and onion over medium heat until beef is no longer pink. Drain; stir in salt and pepper. Transfer beef mixture to a 5-quart slow cooker; stir in tomatoes with juice and remaining ingredients. Cover and cook on low setting for 7 to 9 hours, until vegetables are tender. Discard bay leaf before serving. Makes 7 to 9 servings.

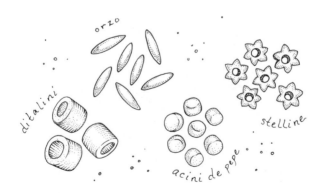

Tiny pasta shapes like ditalini, orzo, acini di pepe and stelline or stars are all quick-cooking and ideal for adding to soup. Choose your favorite...you can even substitute alphabets just for fun.

Working Woman's Chicken Dinner

Beckie Apple
Grannis, AR

Growing up, we had a working mom, and many times she relied on her big slow cooker to help with our supper meal. To feed a family of six, she learned to make large portions. I have cut this recipe down to fit a family of four-plus. It's good served with cooked rice and hot biscuits.

4 boneless or bone-in chicken
    breasts, skin removed
salt and pepper to taste
3 to 4 potatoes, peeled and
    cut into 2-inch cubes
3 to 4 carrots, peeled and cut
    into 2-inch slices

1 onion, cut into large pieces
10-3/4 oz. can cream of
    chicken soup
1-1/4 c. hot water

Arrange chicken in a 5-quart slow cooker; season lightly with salt and pepper. Add vegetables; season lightly with salt and pepper. Whisk together soup and water in a bowl; spoon over all. Cover and cook on high setting for 3 hours. Reduce to low setting and continue cooking for 3 to 4 hours, until chicken and vegetables are tender and cooked through. Serves 4 to 6.

The simplest table decorations are often the prettiest!
Try filling a basket with shiny red apples or fragrant
yellow lemons for the kitchen table.

Chicken, Gravy & Stuffing

Claudia Keller
Carrollton, GA

You're going to want lots of mashed potatoes...
this recipe makes its own savory gravy from the soups.

4 boneless, skinless chicken
   breasts
salt and pepper to taste
1 c. chicken broth
4 to 6 slices Swiss cheese
10-3/4 oz. can cream of
   chicken soup

10-3/4 oz. can cream of
   mushroom soup
1/4 c. milk
2 c. herb-seasoned stuffing
   croutons
1/2 c. butter, melted

Season chicken with salt and pepper; place in a 5-quart slow cooker.
Pour broth around chicken. Top each piece of chicken with a slice of
Swiss cheese. Whisk together soups and milk in a bowl; cover chicken
with soup mixture. Sprinkle stuffing croutons over all; drizzle melted
butter on top. Cover and cook on low setting for 6 to 7 hours, or on
high setting for 3 to 3-1/2 hours. Serves 4.

Favorite Ham Casserole
2c. cooked ham
3c. elbow macaroni
can crm mushroom soup
3/4 c shredded cheddar
1/4 c milk
bread crumbs

Having a potluck party? Ask everyone ahead of time to share
the recipe they'll be bringing. Make copies of all the recipes
and staple into a booklet...a thoughtful party souvenir!

Roast Beef & all the Fixin's

LaDeana Cooper
Batavia, OH

Here's the perfect recipe for when the weather starts to dip and you've got the winter blues, or if you just want a hearty meal waiting for you. It only takes 15 minutes to prep and you're set for a wonderful "belly warmer." If you have any leftovers (which doesn't happen very often at my house), use them to make a quick shepherd pie. Absolutely yummy!

1.35-oz. pkg. onion soup mix
3/4 c. hot water
3 to 3-1/2 lb. beef chuck roast
4 to 6 potatoes, halved
   lengthwise
1-1/2 t. garlic powder

1 t. seasoned salt
1/2 t. pepper
1/2 lb. baby carrots
6 stalks celery, cut into
   2-inch pieces

In a small bowl, stir soup mix into hot water and set aside. Place roast in a 6-quart slow cooker; arrange potatoes around roast. Sprinkle seasonings over roast; top with carrots and celery. Spoon soup mixture over roast and vegetables. Cover and cook on low setting for 8 to 9 hours, or on high setting for 4 hours. Makes 6 to 8 servings.

Tiny, tender new potatoes can simply be placed on top of a roast...they'll steam to perfection while the roast slow-cooks.

Slowly Simmered Flavors
• SLOW COOKER •

Italian Meatloaf

Bunny Palmertree
Carrollton, MS

This is truly an amazing meatloaf recipe. It is so easy to prepare, and the slow cooker does all the work for you. The meatloaf is so flavorful and slices beautifully!

2 slices white bread, torn into
    large pieces
1-1/2 lbs. ground beef chuck
1-1/2 c. mushrooms, finely
    chopped
1 c. shredded mozzarella cheese

1/3 c. pepperoni, finely chopped
1 t. dried oregano
1 t. garlic powder
3/4 t. salt
2 eggs, lightly beaten
2 T. catsup or barbecue sauce

Process bread in a food processor until fine crumbs form. In a large bowl, combine crumbs with remaining ingredients except catsup or barbecue sauce. Mix gently with your hands; form into a 9-inch by 6-inch loaf. Place in a 4-quart slow cooker; brush with catsup or sauce. Cover and cook on low setting for 5 hours. Serves 6.

Creamy Hashbrowns

Patricia Wissler
Harrisburg, PA

These easy potatoes are great served with meatloaf or baked ham, or cook them overnight for a welcome brunch dish.

30-oz. pkg. frozen diced potatoes
2 10-3/4 oz. cans cream of
    chicken soup
1/4 c. butter, melted

16-oz. container French onion
    dip with sour cream
8-oz. pkg. favorite shredded
    cheese

Spread frozen potatoes in an ungreased 5-quart slow cooker. Combine remaining ingredients in a bowl; stir well and spoon over potatoes. Mix well. Cover and cook on low setting for 4 to 5 hours, until potatoes are tender. Serves 10 to 12.

Slow cookers work best when filled
1/2 to 2/3 full.

BBQ Freezer Chicken

Marian Forck
Chamois, MO

My daughter Sarah puts this together ahead of time and freezes it. Then one morning before she leaves for work, she puts it in the slow cooker and it's ready for supper when she gets home. A very handy meal with a working mother and two small children! And you won't spend a lot of time cleaning up the kitchen.

4 boneless, skinless chicken
    breasts
2/3 c. chunky applesauce
2/3 c. barbecue sauce

2 T. brown sugar, packed
1 t. chili powder
1/2 t. pepper

Place chicken in a plastic freezer bag; set aside. Combine remaining ingredients in a small bowl; spoon over chicken, coating well. Seal bag and freeze up to 3 months. To serve, thaw in refrigerator overnight. Spray a 4-quart slow cooker with non-stick vegetable spray, or use a plastic slow-cooker liner; transfer the contents of freezer bag to slow cooker. Cover and cook on low setting for 6 to 8 hours. At serving time, spoon sauce from slow cooker over chicken. Serves 4.

Serve up icy lemonade in frosted-rim glasses. Chill tumblers in the fridge. At serving time, moisten rims with lemon juice or water and dip into a dish of sparkling sugar.

Slowly Simmered Flavors
• SLOW COOKER •

Sweet BBQ Chicken

Lisanne Miller
Wells, ME

*Not spicy, but sweet and smooth! Serve with cornbread
or over mashed potatoes or steamed rice.*

16-oz. bottle favorite barbecue
    sauce
1/2 c. white vinegar
1/2 c. light brown sugar, packed

1 clove garlic, pressed
1/4 c. onion, chopped
2 lbs. boneless, skinless chicken
    breasts

In a bowl, mix together all ingredients except chicken. Spray a 4-quart
slow cooker with non-stick vegetable spray; spoon a thin layer of sauce
mixture into bottom of slow cooker. Arrange chicken in slow cooker; top
with remaining sauce. Cover and cook on low setting for 6 to 7 hours.
Serves 4 to 6.

Tropical BBQ Chicken

Amy Mauseth
Reno, NV

*An easy recipe for a busy family! Serve with jasmine rice
and stir-fry veggies.*

18-oz. bottle barbecue sauce,
    divided
4 boneless, skinless chicken
    breasts

1 t. garlic salt
pepper to taste
20-oz. can pineapple chunks,
    drained and divided

Cover the bottom of a 4-quart slow cooker with a thin layer of sauce;
add 2 chicken breasts. Sprinkle with seasonings; top with half of
pineapple. Repeat layers; add remaining sauce. Cover and cook on
high setting for 5 hours; turn to low setting and cook for 3 hours.
Makes 4 servings.

Slow down and enjoy life.
– Eddie Cantor

Nice & Spicy Pork Ribs

Carol Hickman
Kingsport, TN

This is a nice and easy, and delicious, Sunday dinner. I usually toss these ribs in the slow cooker before leaving for Sunday morning service. Back home after church, I can quickly put together some baked beans, corn on the cob, hot dinner rolls, and if I'm feeling especially generous, a peach cobbler for dessert.

19-oz. bottle spicy original
    barbecue sauce
18-oz. bottle spicy honey
    barbecue sauce

2 to 2-1/2 lbs. country-style
    boneless pork ribs
salt and pepper to taste
1 T. oil

Add both bottles of barbecue sauce to a 5-quart slow cooker; cover and turn to high setting. Season ribs with salt and pepper. Heat oil in a large cast-iron skillet over medium-high heat. Add ribs; brown on both sides, but do not cook through. (For even more flavor, use a hot grill for this step.) Drain ribs on paper towels for several minutes; transfer to slow cooker. Spoon sauce in slow cooker over ribs. Cover and cook on high setting for 3 hours, or on low setting for 4 hours. Uncover for the last hour to allow sauce to thicken. Serves 4 to 6.

Allow a little extra time when slow-cooking in summertime...high humidity can cause food to take longer to finish cooking.

Slowly Simmered Flavors
• SLOW COOKER •

Homestyle Scalloped Potatoes

Donna Carter
Ontario, Canada

My whole family loves the taste of my scalloped potatoes. I like to add extra onions and cheese to bring out the flavor.

6 potatoes, peeled and sliced
3 onions, thinly sliced
12-oz. can evaporated milk
1 c. shredded medium or sharp
    Cheddar cheese
1/4 c. all-purpose flour

1/4 c. celery leaves, chopped
2 T. butter, melted
1 T. dried parsley
1 t. salt
1/2 t. pepper
1/2 t. paprika

In a lightly greased 5-quart slow cooker, layer and alternate potato slices and onion slices. In a bowl, combine remaining ingredients except paprika; mix well and spoon over potato mixture. Sprinkle with paprika. Cover and cook on low setting for 6 to 8 hours. Makes 6 servings.

A slow cooker makes a delightful (and welcome) housewarming or bridal shower gift. Be sure to tie on a few favorite recipes!

Garden-Style Italian Chicken

Mary Shimkus
Glen Ellyn, IL

I'm sort of a country cook...if veggies are involved, I like to add what's in season. Peppers, yellow squash, asparagus, corn, green beans...switch it up and make it yours!

1/2 head cabbage, cut into wedges
1 onion, sliced and separated into rings
4-1/2 oz. jar sliced mushrooms, drained
2 T. quick-cooking tapioca, uncooked

2 to 2-1/2 lbs. chicken breasts, thighs and drumsticks, skin removed
2 c. meatless spaghetti sauce
Garnish: grated Parmesan cheese
Optional: cooked pasta

In a 4-quart slow cooker, combine cabbage wedges, onion and mushrooms. Sprinkle tapioca over vegetables; arrange chicken pieces on top. Pour spaghetti sauce over all. Cover and cook on low setting for 6 to 7 hours, or on high setting for 3 to 3-1/2 hours. Transfer to a serving platter; sprinkle with Parmesan cheese. If desired, serve with hot cooked pasta. Makes 4 to 6 servings.

A rainy day cure-all...toss together ingredients for a tasty slower-cooker meal, make some popcorn and enjoy a family movie marathon. When you're ready for dinner, it's ready for you!

Slowly Simmered Flavors
• SLOW COOKER •

Super-Simple Marinara Sauce

Sheryl Eastman
Keego Harbor, MI

A very simple and quick recipe for a delicious sauce, easy to make in a slow cooker. If you prefer it a little thicker, add some grated Parmesan cheese. If you like it spicy, add a teaspoon of red pepper flakes to make it arrabiata style.

28-oz. can crushed tomatoes
28-oz. can whole tomatoes
2 6-oz. cans tomato paste
2-1/2 T. sugar
1-1/2 t. dried basil

1 t. dried oregano
1 t. salt
1 t. pepper
Optional: 1 T. chopped, dried
    onion or minced garlic

In a 4-quart slow cooker, combine tomatoes with juice and remaining ingredients. Use a potato masher to mash whole tomatoes into bite-size chunks. Cover and cook on low setting for 8 to 10 hours. Sauce tastes even better the next day. Makes 6 servings.

The most indispensable ingredient of
all good home cooking...
love for those you are cooking for.
– Sophia Loren

Tasty Turkey Mac

Dianna Hodnett
Dalton, GA

I make this easy recipe often and rarely do I stick to the exact recipe. My husband and I prefer lots more onions and mushrooms, and I also mix turkey with beef or pork for variations. My husband says he loves all my "conglomerations"...recipes I put together with whatever we have at home!

2 c. elbow macaroni, uncooked
1 t. oil
1-1/2 lbs. ground turkey
15-oz. can corn, drained
4-oz. can sliced mushrooms,
    drained

2 10 3/4-oz. cans tomato soup
1/2 c. onion, chopped
2 T. catsup
1 T. mustard
salt and pepper to taste

Cook macaroni according to package directions, just until tender; drain and transfer to a 5-quart slow cooker. Meanwhile, heat oil in a skillet over medium heat. Cook turkey until browned; drain and add to slow cooker. Add remaining ingredients; stir to blend. Cover and cook on low setting for 7 to 9 hours, or on high setting for 3 to 4 hours. Makes 4 to 6 servings.

Give a busy mom dinner in a dash! Share a favorite recipe along with all the fixin's to prepare it. Then, when time is at a premium, she can toss the ingredients in her slow cooker and forget about cooking.

Slowly Simmered Flavors
• SLOW COOKER •

Mexican Turkey Drumsticks

April Jacobs
Loveland, CO

One Thanksgiving, my husband was away on military duty, and my kids & I didn't feel like having the traditional turkey dinner. I found this recipe, and it was perfect! The kids got to eat their drumsticks with their hands, and we enjoyed Spanish rice and black beans on the side. Such fun...making memories of a different kind!

4 to 6 turkey drumsticks
10-oz. can enchilada sauce
4-oz. can chopped green chiles
1 t. dried oregano

1/2 t. ground cumin
1/2 t. garlic salt
3 T. cornstarch
3 T. cold water

Place drumsticks in a lightly greased 6-quart slow cooker; set aside. Combine remaining ingredients except cornstarch and cold water in a bowl; spoon over drumsticks. Cover and cook on low setting for 8 to 10 hours. Remove drumsticks to a platter; keep warm. Strain sauce in slow cooker into a saucepan. Combine cornstarch and water until smooth; stir into sauce in pan. Bring to a boil over medium heat; cook and stir for 2 minutes, or until thickened. Serve drumsticks with sauce. Serves 4 to 6.

Whip up a zippy Tex-Mex side dish pronto! Prepare instant rice, using chicken broth instead of water. Stir in a generous dollop of spicy salsa, top with shredded cheese and cover until cheese melts.

Gram's Crock Fixin's

Sandy Coffey
Cincinnati, OH

We all think of wintertime as slow-cooker season, but summertime is also a great time for this recipe, when it's extra warm outside. Just set and go! Add hot rolls and a tossed salad for a real country-style dinner, and a sprinkle of shredded cheese, if you want to dress it up.

2 lbs. cooked ham, cubed	4 redskin potatoes, cubed
2 lbs. fresh green beans, snapped, or 3 14-1/2 oz. cans green beans, drained	1 onion, diced
	3 c. water
	salt and pepper to taste

Combine all ingredients in a 5-quart slow cooker. Cover and cook on low setting for 6 hours, or until potatoes and beans are tender. Makes 4 to 6 servings.

Just for fun, serve up soft pretzels instead of dinner rolls... so easy, the kids can do it! Twist strips of refrigerated bread stick dough into pretzel shapes and place on an ungreased baking sheet. Brush with beaten egg white, sprinkle with coarse salt and bake as the package directs.

Ultimate Creamed Corn

Marsha Baker
Pioneer, OH

The first time I tasted this wonderful dish, my reaction was, "Wow!" Amazing, creamy and always a hit. It's sure to become your favorite after one bite too.

2 16-oz. pkgs. frozen corn	2 t. sugar or sugar substitute
1-1/2 c. cream cheese, cubed	1 t. salt
3/4 c. milk	1/4 t. pepper
6 to 8 T. butter, melted	

Spray a 4-quart slow cooker with cooking spray. Add corn and spread over the bottom. Push cream cheese cubes into the center of the corn; set aside. In a small bowl, stir together remaining ingredients; spoon over top. Cover and cook on high setting for 2 hours. Stir well before serving. Corn will hold on low setting up to one hour; stir occasionally. Makes 6 to 8 servings.

Need 1/2 cup cream cheese for a recipe? No need to mess up a measuring cup...just slice an 8-ounce package in half. Each half equals 1/2 cup.

Vickie's Pork Carnitas

Vickie Wiseman
Hamilton, OH

This is a slow-cooker version of carnitas, a traditional Mexican filling of shredded pork. The recipe features its rich flavor and tenderness without the usual messy frying. I like to make up packets of the seasoning mix to keep on hand...they make great little gifts to present to friends.

1 T. chili powder
2 t. ground cumin
2 t. garlic powder
1-1/2 t. salt
1 t. onion powder

2 lbs. boneless pork tenderloin
8 8-inch flour tortillas or corn
   taco shells
Garnish: favorite toppings

Combine all seasonings in a small bowl. Coat pork with spice mixture; place in a 4-quart slow cooker. No liquid needs to be added. Cover and cook on low setting for 8 to 10 hours, or on high setting for 4 to 5 hours, until pork is tender enough to shred. Remove pork to a plate, reserving juices in slow cooker. Shred pork with 2 forks, discarding fat; stir enough of reserved juices into pork to moisten. (If desired, make pork 2 days ahead, cover and refrigerate. Reserve juices separately, removing any fat that hardens on surface. Reheat pork with juices.) Serve with tortillas and desired toppings. Serves 8.

Mix up some flavorful homemade salsa. Combine a 14-1/2 ounce can of diced tomatoes with green chiles, 1/2 cup diced onion, a minced garlic clove and a tablespoon of lime juice. Enjoy it chunky style, or for a smoother consistency, place in a food processor and pulse 2 to 3 times.

Charlene's Beef Tostadas

Charlene McCain
Bakersfield, CA

Got a busy weekend ahead? This is the perfect dish to make. Spend just a little time in the kitchen getting the ingredients ready, turn on the slow cooker and go about your business until dinnertime. Serve with a chopped salad and fresh fruit.

1 lb. ground beef
1 c. onion, chopped
1/2 c. green pepper, chopped
10-oz. can diced tomatoes with
   green chiles
2 16-oz. cans pinto beans,
   drained and rinsed
1/3 c. water

1/2 t. chili powder
1/2 t. ground cumin
1/2 t. salt
1/4 t. pepper
6 6-inch flour tortillas
8-oz. pkg. shredded Cheddar or
   Monterey cheese, divided

In a large skillet over medium heat, brown beef with onion and green pepper; drain. Add undrained tomatoes and remaining ingredients except cheese and tortillas; bring to a boil. Reduce heat to low; cover and simmer for 10 minutes. In a 5-quart slow cooker, layer 3/4 cup beef mixture, one tortilla and 1/3 cup cheese. Repeat layers, ending with cheese. Cover and cook on low setting for 5 to 7 hours. Serves 4.

Homemade guacamole is scrumptious, and it's oh-so easy to make. Cut 4 ripe avocados in half, remove the pits and scoop into a bowl. Add a chopped onion, 2 minced cloves of garlic, 2 tablespoons of lime juice and a dash of salt. Mash it up and serve with crisp tortilla chips...it can't be beat!

Sunshine Pork Chops

Janis Parr
Ontario, Canada

This is a perfect dish to serve to company. It looks and tastes amazing! I serve it with creamy mashed potatoes and steamed fresh vegetables.

5 to 6 bone-in pork chops
salt and pepper to taste
2 T. oil
29-oz. can cling peach slices,
    drained and 1/4 c. syrup
    reserved

8-oz. can tomato sauce
1/4 c. brown sugar, packed
1/4 c. vinegar
1/2 t. cinnamon
1/8 t. ground cloves

Season pork chops with salt and pepper. Heat oil in a skillet over medium heat; brown pork chops on both sides. Drain; transfer pork chops to a 5-quart slow cooker. Arrange peach slices on top. Combine reserved peach syrup and remaining ingredients in a bowl; mix well and spoon over peaches. Cover and cook on low setting for 6 to 8 hours, or on high setting for 3 to 4 hours. Makes 5 to 6 servings.

Sweet potatoes, carrots, parsnips, onions and other root vegetables grow tender and sweet when slow-cooked. Just load up the slow cooker with veggie chunks, drizzle with a little honey and olive oil and cook on low for 4 to 6 hours, until tender. Season with salt and pepper.

Slowly Simmered Flavors
• SLOW COOKER •

Tomato-Soy Pork Chops

Elaine Mathis
Marion, IN

My "I hate pork" grandson loves these!

1/4 c. all-purpose flour
1/4 t. garlic powder
1/4 t. pepper
6 boneless pork chops
1/4 c. oil

3 T. soy sauce
1/3 c. water
1 onion, thinly sliced
14-1/2 oz. can diced tomatoes,
   drained

Combine flour and seasonings in a plastic zipping bag; add pork chops and shake to coat. Heat oil in a large skillet over medium heat; brown pork chops on both sides. Drain; transfer to a 5-quart slow cooker. Top with remaining ingredients. Cover and cook on low setting for 3 to 3-1/2 hours, until pork chops are tender. Makes 6 servings.

No-Worries Pork Chops

Shirl Parsons
Cape Carteret, NC

This is my own original recipe...the foil cooking yields juicy, tender pork chops every time. They're also good with Italian seasoning, garlic powder and onion powder.

4 to 6 assorted pork chops
salt and pepper to taste

ground sage and ground cumin
   to taste

Lay each pork chop on a piece of aluminum foil; season as desired. Fold up the sides and ends of foil; seal well to make packets. Layer packets in a 5-quart slow cooker; no need to add any liquid. Cover and cook on low setting for 6 to 8 hrs. Makes 4 to 6 servings.

A speedy side...stir-fry frozen green beans in a little olive oil until crisp-tender. Toss with a jar of roasted red peppers.

Beans & Wieners

Sharon Leach
Two Rivers, WI

A picnic favorite! Try some variations too...use Italian-seasoned tomatoes for a different flavor, omit the hot dogs and add 1/2 cup crisp crumbled bacon or omit the tomato sauce for a less juicy dish.

1 lb. hot dogs, each cut into 4 pieces
14-1/2 oz. can stewed tomatoes, cut up
16-oz. can vegetarian baked beans
15-1/2 oz. can butter beans, drained and rinsed
15-oz. can red kidney beans, drained and rinsed

15-oz. can lima beans, drained and rinsed
8-oz. can tomato sauce with basil, oregano and garlic
1 c. carrots, peeled and thinly sliced
1 c. onion, chopped
1/2 t. garlic salt
1/8 t. cayenne pepper

In a 4-quart slow cooker, combine hot dogs, tomatoes with juice, baked beans with juice and remaining ingredients. Mix well. Cover and cook on high setting for 4 hours. Serves 6 to 8.

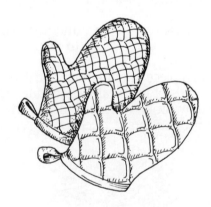

Keep a pair of long padded oven mitts nearby when slow cooking. They're perfect for lifting and carrying the hot crock safely.

Slowly Simmered Flavors
• SLOW COOKER •

Potato Tot Casserole

Emilie Britton
New Bremen, OH

*Who doesn't like an easy-peasy recipe? This smells
so good and tastes good too!*

32-oz. pkg. frozen potato puffs
1 lb. ground beef, browned
   and drained
2 14-1/2 oz. cans green beans,
   drained
10-3/4 oz. can cream of
   mushroom soup

1 T. dried, chopped onion
1/4 c. milk
1/2 t. salt
1/4 t. pepper

Line a 5-quart slow cooker with frozen potato puffs. Combine remaining
ingredients in a bowl; spoon over potatoes. Cover and cook on high
setting for 3 hours. Makes 6 to 8 servings.

Start a tradition of having a regular night for dinner guests.
Many slow-cooker recipes make plenty of food for sharing.
Invite a neighbor or co-worker you've wanted to get to
know better...encourage your kids to invite a friend.
You'll be so glad you did!

Honey Pork Roast

Cindy Neel
Gooseberry Patch

My family & friends love this roast, and it's a snap to make. I like to serve it with baked sweet potatoes and buttered broccoli.

3 to 4-lb. bone-in pork loin roast	2 T. dried basil
2/3 c. grated Parmesan cheese	2 T. olive oil
1/2 c. honey	2 T. garlic, minced
1/4 c. soy sauce	3/4 t. salt
2 T. dried oregano	1/2 t. pepper

Place pork roast in a 5-quart slow cooker; set aside. Combine remaining ingredients in a small bowl; mix well and spoon over roast. Cover and cook on low setting for 6 to 8 hours. Remove roast to a platter; reserve liquid in slow cooker. Shred roast with 2 forks; cover to keep warm. Transfer reserved cooking liquid to a saucepan; bring to a boil over medium heat. Reduce heat to medium-low; simmer until thickened and reduced. To serve, ladle sauce over shredded pork. Serves 6 to 8.

A tasty apple coleslaw goes well with pork. Simply toss together a large bag of coleslaw mix, a chopped Granny Smith apple and coleslaw dressing or mayonnaise to taste.

Slowly Simmered Flavors
• SLOW COOKER •

Country Green Beans & Bacon
Megan Brooks
Antioch, TN

My grandma used to have these beans cooking all day on the back of the stove. This way tastes just as good, but is so much easier!

10 to 12 slices bacon
2 lbs. fresh green beans, ends
   trimmed
1/2 c. yellow onion, chopped

2 cloves garlic, minced
1 T. olive oil
3/4 c. chicken broth
1/8 t. salt, or to taste

In a skillet over medium heat, cook bacon until nearly crisp. Remove bacon to a paper towel; set aside 1/4 cup drippings. In the same skillet, sauté onion and garlic in oil just until tender. Combine bacon, reserved drippings, onion mixture, broth and salt in a 4-quart slow cooker. Cover and cook on low setting for 6 to 8 hours. Serves 6.

Smashed Garlic Potatoes
Jess Brunink
Whitehall, MI

This is a family favorite. It's great to make for get-togethers and holidays, because you can make it ahead, and then put it in your slow cooker.

4 lbs. redskin potatoes, cubed
1 T. salt
salt to taste
2 cloves garlic, minced

1/2 c. butter
10-3/4 oz. can cream of
   mushroom soup

In a saucepan, cover potatoes with water; add one tablespoon salt and bring to a boil. Cook until fork-tender; drain and return to pot. Mash potatoes; stir in salt to taste, garlic, butter and soup. Transfer to a greased 4-quart slow cooker. Cover and cook on low setting setting for 3 to 5 hours. Makes 8 to 10 servings.

Prefer not to leave a slow cooker on while you're away? Simple...put it to work overnight! In the morning, refrigerate food in a fridge container. Reheat at suppertime.

Cheesy Chicken Spaghetti

Marsha Baker
Pioneer, OH

This simple dish is such comfort food. It's always great when the slow cooker can do the work for you and dinner is ready when you get home from running errands. The recipe can easily be cut in half...but why not tuck the leftovers into the freezer, for an easy meal another day? Use low-fat products if you like.

16-oz. pkg. spaghetti, uncooked
1 lb. pasteurized process
   cheese, cubed
1-1/2 c. cooked chicken, diced,
   or 12-1/2 oz. can chicken
   breast, drained and flaked
10-3/4 oz. can cream of
   chicken soup
10-3/4 oz. can cream of
   mushroom soup

10-oz. can diced tomatoes with
   green chiles
4-oz. can mushroom stems and
   pieces, drained
1/2 c. water
1/2 c. onion, diced
salt and pepper to taste
Optional: 1 green pepper, diced

Cook spaghetti according to package instructions, just until tender; drain. Spray a 6-quart slow cooker with non-stick vegetable spray. Combine spaghetti and remaining ingredients in slow cooker; stir to mix well. Cover and cook on low setting for 2 to 3 hours, until hot and bubbly. Stir again just before serving. Serves 10 to 12.

A hearty dish like Cheesy Chicken Spaghetti is perfect on a cool autumn night. Carry the crock right out to your backyard picnic table, and savor the fall colors with your family!

Slowly Simmered Flavors
• SLOW COOKER •

Mom's Lasagna

Christina Addison
Blanchester, OH

*My mom used to make lasagna when I was little, and it was
one of my favorites. Over the years, I've transformed it into
a slow-cooker version to make it easier to prepare.*

1 lb. ground beef
1/2 c. onion, diced
24-oz. jar spaghetti sauce
2 T. dried parsley
1 t. dried oregano
1/2 t. ground bay leaf

15-oz. container ricotta cheese
8-oz. pkg. shredded mozzarella
  cheese, divided
1 egg, beaten
16-oz. pkg. oven-ready lasagna
  noodles, uncooked

In a skillet over medium heat, cook beef and onion until beef is no
longer pink. Drain; stir in spaghetti sauce and seasonings. In a bowl,
combine ricotta cheese, one cup mozzarella cheese and egg; set aside. In
a greased 4-quart slow cooker, spread some of sauce mixture to lightly
cover the bottom. Add several lasagna noodles, breaking in half to fit
as necessary. Spread noodles with more sauce and some of remaining
mozzarella cheese. Drop some of the ricotta mixture on top by
teaspoonfuls. Repeat layering, saving some mozzarella cheese and
ricotta cheese for the top. Cover and cook on low setting for 4 to
5 hours. Makes 8 servings.

Whip up some delicious Parmesan bread! Split an Italian loaf in
half and spread with a mixture of 1/4 cup butter, 2 tablespoons
grated Parmesan cheese, 2 teaspoons minced garlic and
1/4 teaspoon oregano. Broil until bubbly and golden.

Italian Pot Roast

Amanda Lusignolo
Gooseberry Patch

My family loves my tried & true roast from the slow cooker,
but I wanted to try something different. This is easy and flavorful.
I like to serve it with bowtie pasta and sliced zucchini.

1/2 lb. sliced mushrooms
1 sweet onion, halved and sliced
2 T. olive oil
3 to 4-lb. boneless chuck roast,
    fat trimmed
14-1/2 oz. can beef broth
8-oz. can tomato sauce

1.35-oz. pkg. onion soup mix
1 t. pepper
3 T. tomato paste
1 t. Italian seasoning
2 T. cornstarch
2 T. cold water

In a greased 6-quart slow cooker, combine mushrooms and onion; set aside. Heat oil in a heavy skillet over medium-high heat. Add roast and brown on all sides. Remove roast to slow cooker. Pour broth and tomato sauce over roast; sprinkle with soup mix and pepper. Cover and cook on low setting for 8 to 10 hours, until roast shreds easily with a fork. Transfer roast to a cutting board; cut into large chunks. Cover with aluminum foil to keep warm. Skim fat from juices in slow cooker; stir in tomato paste and Italian seasoning. Stir together cornstarch and cold water in a cup until smooth; add to juices in slow cooker, stirring until blended. Cover and cook on high setting for 40 minutes, or until mixture is thickened. Stir in roast; heat through. Serves 6.

Dress up a tossed green salad with this simple vinaigrette dressing. In a small jar, combine 2 tablespoons cider vinegar and 6 tablespoons olive oil; twist on the lid and shake well. Stir in a teaspoon of Dijon mustard or minced fresh basil...season with salt and pepper. Delicious!

Mary Ann's Roast Beef

Patricia Harris
Hendersonville, TN

A special neighbor of my in-laws took this roast to their house when we had a loss in the family. We were all in from out of town and so appreciated this scrumptious warm meal.

2 T. oil
3-lb. beef chuck roast
2 c. water
1-oz. pkg. Italian salad
    dressing mix

1-oz. pkg. ranch salad dressing
    mix
1-oz. pkg. brown gravy mix

Heat oil in a heavy skillet over medium-high heat. Brown roast on all sides; remove to a 4-quart slow cooker. Whisk together remaining ingredients in a bowl; drizzle over roast. Cover and cook on low setting for 8 hours, or on high setting for 4 hours. Makes 6 to 8 servings.

Set up a framed menu at your next gathering...let everyone know that delicious dishes like "Great-Grandmother's Pot Roast" and "Aunt Betty's Pudding Cake" await!

Chicken Broc-Cauli Casserole
Courtney Stultz
Weir, KS

Chicken with broccoli & rice is one of our favorite comfort food dishes. This is an easy version for the slow cooker, using cauliflower "rice" to make it low-carb. Save time by putting your food processor to work, chopping veggies.

3 boneless, skinless chicken
    breasts, cubed
1 head cauliflower, finely
    chopped
1 bunch broccoli, finely chopped
1 c. carrots, peeled and finely
    chopped
1/2 lb. mushrooms, finely
    chopped

1 onion, finely chopped
1 c. chicken broth
1/2 c. cream cheese, softened
2 T. olive oil
2 t. ground sage
1 t. sea salt
1/2 t. pepper
1 c. favorite shredded cheese

In a 5-quart slow cooker, combine chicken and vegetables; set aside. In a small bowl, whisk together broth, cream cheese, oil and seasonings; spoon over chicken mixture. Mix well and top with shredded cheese. Cover and cook on high setting for about 4 hours. Makes 6 servings.

Add a crunchy golden crumb topping to slow-cooked casseroles. Sauté soft fresh bread crumbs in a little butter or olive oil and sprinkle them on the casserole just before serving.

Chicken & White Beans

Kristin Stone
Little Elm, TX

I wanted to create a fiber-packed dish that my husband would enjoy. This meal is easy to make in your slow cooker and packs in 16 grams of fiber per serving! Chock-full of chicken and beans, it's the perfect meal. My husband wanted me to add that it's best topped with a spoonful of salsa...gives it kick!

1 lb. dried Great Northern beans, rinsed and sorted
4 c. reduced-sodium chicken broth
1 onion, chopped
1-1/8 t. garlic, minced
2 t. ground cumin
1-1/2 t. dried oregano
1 t. ground coriander
1/8 t. ground cloves
1/8 t. cayenne pepper
4-oz. can chopped green chiles
1 c. cooked chicken breast, cubed
1/2 link turkey or pork Kielbasa sausage, sliced

Soak beans in water overnight; drain. Place beans in a 5-quart slow cooker. Cover beans with broth; add onion, garlic and seasonings. Mix together. Cover and cook on low setting for 7 to 8 hours. Stir in chiles, chicken and kielbasa; cover and cook for one additional hour. Serves 6.

Cook once, eat twice! Make a double batch and save half in a freezer-safe container; freeze up to 3 months. Thaw overnight in the fridge...reheat in a saucepan or in the microwave. Some busy day, you'll be so glad to have it!

Deb's Cashew Chicken

Debbie Deverill
Gilbert, AZ

I was house-sitting for some dear friends and wanted to have supper ready for them when they got home. My family loves this recipe, so I made it for my friends and they loved it too. Fix some white or brown rice, and dinner is ready.

10-3/4 oz. can cream of
    mushroom or chicken soup
1 lb. fresh bean sprouts, or
    14-oz. can bean sprouts,
    drained
1 c. celery, sliced
4-oz. can sliced mushrooms,
    drained
1/2 c. green onions, chopped
3 T. butter, sliced
1 T. soy sauce
4 to 6 boneless, skinless chicken
    breasts
1 c. whole cashews
cooked rice

In a 6-quart slow cooker, combine all ingredients except chicken, cashews and rice; stir. Add chicken; push into soup mixture. Cover and cook on low setting for 4 to 6 hours, or on high setting for 2 to 3 hours, until chicken is cooked through. Stir in cashews just before serving. Serve chicken and vegetable mixture over cooked rice. Makes 4 to 6 servings.

After a simple dinner, a sweet & simple dessert is in order.
Place scoops of rainbow sherbet in parfait glasses and slip
a fortune cookie over the edge of each glass...perfect!

Beef Chow Mein

Annette Ingram
Grand Rapids, MI

A good old-fashioned Chinese restaurant favorite to make at home. My kids love it when I pick up a box of fortune cookies to open afterwards!

2 to 3 t. oil
1 lb. beef round steak, cut into
   cubes or strips
3 T. soy sauce
1 c. beef broth
28-oz. can chop suey vegetables,
   drained
14-oz. can bean sprouts, drained

6-oz. jar sliced mushrooms,
   drained
1 onion, diced
1 stalk celery, diced
3 T. cornstarch
1/2 c. cold water
cooked rice or chow mein
   noodles

Heat oil in a skillet over medium heat. Add beef and brown on all sides. Drain; transfer to a 4-quart slow cooker. Add soy sauce, broth and all vegetables; mix well. Cover and cook on low setting for 7 to 8 hours, until beef is tender. Combine cornstarch and cold water in a cup; mix well and stir into beef mixture. Cover and cook until sauce is thickened, 15 to 20 minutes. Serve beef mixture over cooked rice or noodles. Serves 4.

Host an adventure potluck! Ask each guest to bring a favorite dish from "back home"...whether that's somewhere across the USA, or halfway around the world.

Slow-Cooked Stuffed Peppers

LaDeana Cooper
Batavia, OH

Who wants to fix dinner after coming home from work? Do a little prep, turn on the slow cooker and have dinner waiting for you! Either small or medium-size peppers work best.

6 to 8 green, red or yellow
  peppers
2-1/2 to 3 lbs. ground beef
2 eggs, beaten
1/2 c. sweet onion, diced
1 c. quick-cooking rice, uncooked
1 T. dried parsley, or 3 T. fresh
  parsley, chopped

1 t. seasoned salt
1-1/2 t. pepper, divided
3 t. garlic, minced and divided
3 T. tomato paste
14-1/2 oz. can diced tomatoes
1-1/2 t. salt
1 t. dried oregano

Cut off tops of peppers, about 1/2-inch down from top. Remove the seeds and ribs; rinse. Finely dice the pepper tops; set aside. In a large bowl, combine beef and eggs. Add diced pepper, onion, rice, parsley, seasoned salt, 1/2 teaspoon pepper and 2 teaspoons garlic. Mix well. Fill peppers with beef mixture, 1/2 to one cup per pepper, filling to the top of peppers. Arrange peppers in a large slow cooker; cut-side up. In a separate bowl, whisk tomato paste into undrained diced tomatoes. Add salt, oregano and remaining pepper and garlic; stir well. Spoon sauce over peppers. Cover and cook on low setting for 8 hours, or on high setting for 4 hours. Serves 6 to 8.

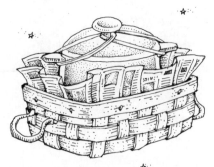

Carrying a filled slow cooker to a party can be tricky. To keep the lid secure, slip a large rubber band under one handle, twist it around the knob on the lid and wrap under the other handle.

Slowly Simmered Flavors
• SLOW COOKER •

Can't-Fail Beef & Mushrooms

Lisa Cunningham
Boothbay, ME

I've been making this dish for years...you can't mess it up! It's a great recipe for new cooks. A yummy dish to serve on a cold, snowy day, great served over mashed potatoes or cooked egg noodles. Serve with garlic bread or hot biscuits.

1 onion, thinly sliced
2 lbs. beef round steak, cut into
   2-inch cubes
10-3/4 oz. can cream of
   mushroom soup

1-1/4 c. milk
1.35-oz. pkg. onion soup mix
3/4 lb. mushrooms, halved

Spray a 4-quart slow cooker with non-stick vegetable spray. Layer onion slices in the bottom; top with beef cubes. In a bowl, whisk together soup and milk; spoon over beef. Sprinkle soup mix over all; do not stir. Cover and cook on low setting for 8 hours, or on high setting for 4 hours. During the last hour, add mushrooms; push down into sauce. Makes 4 to 6 servings.

Flavors sometimes grow milder over a long cooking time.
If that happens, simply add some chopped fresh herbs or
a dash of lemon juice or balsamic vinegar to the dish
to brighten the flavors.

Cowboy Calico Beans

Lindsey Chrostowski
Janesville, WI

Always a hit at get-togethers! This is a recipe that was handed down to me. I tweaked it and made my own variations.

1 lb. ground beef
1 lb. bacon
32-oz. can pork & beans
16-oz. can butter beans, drained
16-oz. can kidney beans, drained
1 red onion, diced
1 green pepper, diced
1 red pepper, diced

Optional: 11-oz. can sweet corn
    & diced peppers, drained
1 c. catsup
1/2 c. brown sugar, packed
1 t. vinegar
1 T. molasses
salt and pepper to taste

In a large skillet over medium heat, brown beef. Drain and transfer to a 5-quart slow cooker. In the same skillet, cook bacon. Drain on paper towels; crumble and add to beef. Add undrained pork & beans and remaining ingredients; mix well. Cover and cook on high setting for one hour. Turn slow cooker to low setting and cook for an additional 2 to 4 hours. Makes 8 to 10 servings.

Keep a big stack of colorful bandannas on hand for casual meals. You can use some as napkins, add one to the bread basket to keep rolls warm and layer the rest down the center of the table for a quick runner.

Slowly Simmered Flavors
• SLOW COOKER •

BBQ Beef Brisket

Diane Cohen
Breinigsville, PA

Need to feed a crowd? This recipe will make a lot of people very happy! Serve with toasty rolls, coleslaw and potato salad for a wonderful meal.

5 to 6-lb. beef brisket
2 c. catsup
3/4 c. regular or non-alcoholic
    beer
1/2 c. brown sugar, packed

1/2 c. Worcestershire sauce
1/2 c. cider vinegar
4 cloves garlic, minced
1 t. salt

Place brisket in a large glass or plastic food container; set aside. For sauce, combine remaining ingredients in a saucepan. Bring to a boil over medium heat; reduce heat to low and simmer for 10 minutes. Pour sauce over brisket; cover and refrigerate for several hours or overnight to marinate. Transfer brisket to a 6-quart slow cooker; pour sauce over brisket. Cover and cook on low setting for 9 to 10 hours, until very tender. Remove brisket to a platter; let stand for 10 minutes. Thinly slice brisket across the grain; serve with sauce from slow cooker. Makes 10 to 12 servings.

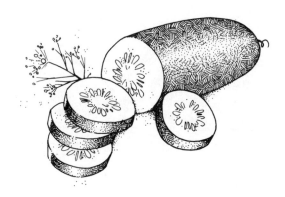

A garden-fresh side dish that's ready in a jiffy. Beat together one cup sour cream, 2 tablespoons vinegar and 4 tablespoons sugar. Fold in one to 2 peeled and thinly sliced cucumbers; season with salt and pepper. Chill until serving time.

Rib-Eye Steak Dinner

Jewel Sharpe
Raleigh, NC

A really delicious recipe and a great one-pot meal! Treat yourself if you're going to be out all day, whether at work or at play.

1-1/2 to 2 lbs. beef rib-eye steak
Montreal steak seasoning to taste
1/4 c. chicken broth
2 T. Worcestershire sauce
2 baking potatoes

1 sweet onion, peeled
Optional: butter and honey
    to taste
2 to 4 ears sweet corn, husks
    removed

Rub steaks with seasoning. Place seasoned steaks in a 6-quart slow cooker; drizzle with broth and Worcestershire sauce. Pierce potatoes several times with a fork; wrap each potato in aluminum foil and add to slow cooker. Hollow out onion; spoon in some butter and honey in the center of the onion. (This step is optional.) Wrap onion in foil; add to slow cooker. Wrap each ear of corn in foil and add to cooker. Slow cooker will be quite full. Cover and cook on low setting for 8 to 9 hours, or on high setting for 5 to 7 hours. Serves 2 to 4.

Take along the slow cooker on your next RV or camping trip! Put dinner on to cook in the morning, then sit down to a hearty home-cooked meal after a day of hiking, fishing or other vacation fun.

Slowly Simmered Flavors
• SLOW COOKER •

One-Pot Ranch Pork Chop Meal

Julie Dossantos
Fort Pierce, FL

Slow-cooker cooking is so easy! This recipe is my take on a familiar one, and it takes just minutes to put it together...let the kids help! Adding lots of veggies gives your family a healthy, complete meal. Serve with warm rolls.

1/2 yellow onion, sliced and
    divided
1-1/2 c. baby carrots, divided
1-1/2 c. sliced mushrooms,
    divided
1-1/2 c. Yukon gold potatoes,
    cubed and divided

2 10-3/4 oz. cans low-fat cream
    of celery soup, divided
1-oz. pkg. ranch salad dressing
    mix, divided
4 boneless pork chops

In a 5-quart slow cooker, layer half each of all vegetables. Spread 1/2 of one can of soup over vegetables; sprinkle with 1/4 of salad dressing mix. Top with pork chops. Spoon remaining 1/2 can of soup over pork chops; sprinkle with another 1/4 of dressing mix. Add remaining vegetables, soup and dressing mix. Cover and cook on low setting for 6 to 7 hours, until vegetables and pork chops are tender. Makes 4 servings.

An easy way to thicken a slow-cooker recipe that's too saucy...remove the lid and cook on high setting for the final 30 minutes of cooking time.

Lemon-Pepper Chicken

Beth Wallace
Canton, GA

I am a busy working mom of three. Any time I can toss a meal in the slow cooker before I leave for work, I am all for it! My husband likes this dish too. I like using the slow-cooker liners for an even easier clean-up. This makes a very nice gravy.

2 lbs. boneless, skinless chicken
   breasts
12-oz. bottle lemon pepper
   marinade

10-3/4 oz. can cream of
   chicken soup
1/2 c. plus 2 T. water
1 c. long-cooking rice, cooked

Place chicken in a 4-quart slow cooker. Add marinade to cover and coat chicken. Cover and cook on low setting for 4 to 6 hours, until chicken is falling-apart tender. Remove chicken from slow cooker. Add soup and water to liquid in slow cooker; stir together. Return chicken to slow cooker; mix well. To serve, stir rice into mixture in slow cooker, or spoon chicken and gravy mixture over rice. Makes 4 servings.

Scalloped Chicken

Sherri Tulini
Pitman, NJ

Who can say no to chicken, cheese and potatoes? With this family favorite, you'll never have any leftovers!

4 boneless, skinless chicken
   breasts
5-oz. pkg. scalloped potato mix
10-oz. pkg. frozen baby peas

2 c. chicken broth
10-3/4 oz. can Cheddar cheese
   soup

Place chicken in a 4-quart slow cooker. Add potatoes, seasoning packet from mix and peas. Combine soup and broth in a bowl; pour over all. Cover and cook on low setting for 7 to 8 hours, or on high setting for 3-1/2 to 4 hours. Serves 4.

Slowly Simmered Flavors
• SLOW COOKER •

Italian Chicken & Rice

Diane Cohen
Breinigsville, PA

Since finding this recipe a few years ago, I have made it many times. It's easy as well as really tasty, and I always have the ingredients on hand. Just add some steamed broccoli for a delicious dinner.

10-3/4 oz. can cream of
  chicken soup
8-oz. pkg. cream cheese,
  softened
0.7-oz. pkg. Italian salad
  dressing mix

5 to 6 boneless, skinless
  chicken breasts
cooked rice

In a lightly greased 5-quart slow cooker, mix together soup, cream cheese and salad dressing mix. Add chicken; turn to coat with soup mixture. Cover and cook on low setting for 6 to 8 hours, until chicken is very tender. Stir, breaking up chicken into small pieces. Serve over cooked rice. Serves 5 to 6.

Savory Chicken & Sweet Potatoes

Ashley Billings
Fort Worth, TX

This is a slow-cooker family favorite!

1 onion, thinly sliced
4 to 5 sweet potatoes, peeled and
  cubed
4 boneless, skinless chicken
  breasts

10-3/4 oz. can cream of
  mushroom soup
1/2 t. dried marjoram

Arrange onion slices in a 5-quart slow cooker; add sweet potatoes and chicken. Spread soup on top; sprinkle with marjoram. Cover and cook on low setting for 7 to 8 hours. Serves 4.

Enlist slow cookers as a handy holiday helper! If there's a turkey in the oven, simply fill 'em up with potatoes, dressing and other sides to cook on the countertop.

Mac & Cheese with Bacon

Marlene Burns
Sebring, FL

This was always a favorite when I was growing up on the farm.

4 c. elbow macaroni or other
    pasta, uncooked
8 slices bacon, crisply cooked
    and divided
2 c. whole milk
12-oz. can evaporated milk
2 t. Dijon mustard

1 t. onion powder
1/4 t. salt
1/4 t. pepper
6-oz. pkg. thin-sliced deli-style
    American cheese, chopped
1 c. shredded Gouda cheese

Coat a 5-quart slow cooker with non-stick vegetable spray. Cook macaroni according to package directions, but 2 minutes less than stated on package; drain. Meanwhile, crumble 6 slices bacon into slow cooker; add milks, mustard and seasonings. Whisk until blended. Add macaroni; toss to coat. Cover and cook on low setting for 2-1/2 hours. Stir in cheeses; cover and cook an additional 30 minutes. Just before serving, crumble reserved bacon on top. Makes 6 servings.

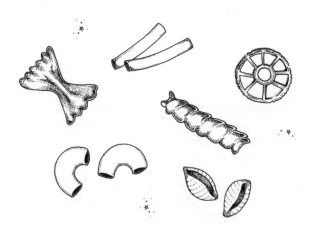

Try using a different shape of pasta next time you make macaroni & cheese. Cavatappi, seashells and bow ties all hold cheese sauce well...they're fun for kids too!

Slowly Simmered Flavors
• SLOW COOKER •

Oh-So-Easy Baked Ham

Nancy Wise
Little Rock, AR

This recipe couldn't be any easier, and it's delicious! Slice and serve hot for dinner, or cool for a sandwich buffet.

3 to 4-lb. cooked boneless ham   10-oz. jar cherry ham glaze
1/2 c. water

Wrap ham in a long sheet of aluminum foil; leave unsealed on top. Add water to a 4-quart slow cooker; add ham. Spoon glaze over ham and fold over foil to seal. Cover and cook on low setting for 6 to 7 hours, until heated through. Remove ham to a platter; remove foil and slice to serve. Makes 12 to 14 servings.

Candied Sweet Potatoes

Claire Bertram
Lexington, KY

Just like Grandma used to make...but easier!

4 to 5 sweet potatoes, peeled and   zest and juice of 1 orange
   cubed   1-1/2 t. cinnamon
3/4 c. light brown sugar, packed   1/2 t. vanilla extract
1/4 c. honey   1/8 t. nutmeg
1/4 c. butter, sliced

Add sweet potatoes to a lightly greased 4-quart slow cooker. Combine remaining ingredients in a saucepan. Cook and stir over medium heat until brown sugar is dissolved. Spoon mixture over sweet potatoes. Cover and cook on low setting for 6 to 8 hours, until potatoes are tender. Serves 6 to 8.

Plug your slow cooker into an automatic timer if you need it to start cooking while you're away. Well-chilled foods can safely be held at room temperature up to 2 hours.

Greek Chicken Gyros

Lori Rosenberg
University Heights, OH

To keep dinners interesting, I like to prepare a variety of international foods for my family. This is a great go-to for that culinary trip to Greece.

2 lbs. boneless, skinless
    chicken breasts
3 T. olive oil
1 T. red wine vinegar
juice of 1/2 lemon
1/3 c. water
2 cloves garlic, minced
1 t. dried oregano
1/2 t. dried dill weed

1/8 t. red pepper flakes
1/2 t. salt
1/2 t. pepper
8 pita rounds or soft flour
    tortillas
12-oz. container tzatziki sauce
Garnish: sliced red onion, sliced
    grape tomatoes, crumbled
    feta cheese

Spray a 4-quart slow cooker with non-stick vegetable spray; add chicken and set aside. In a bowl, combine oil, vinegar, lemon juice, water, garlic and seasonings; whisk well and pour over chicken. Cover and cook on low setting for 6 to 8 hours, or on high setting for 4 to 6 hours, until chicken is very tender. Remove chicken to a platter; shred with 2 forks. To serve, divide chicken among pita rounds or tortillas. Serve topped with tzatziki sauce, onion, tomatoes and cheese. Serves 4, 2 gyros each.

Headed outside for a backyard party? Grab a wicker garden caddy...fill it up with napkins, condiments and everything you need!

French Dip Sandwiches

Karen Shankle
Sacramento, CA

This recipe was given to me by a friend. It's so easy to make and so tasty. My roommates and I absolutely love it!

2-1/2 lbs. beef round steak or
    London broil, fat trimmed
4-1/2 c. water
1 c. soy sauce
2 t. dried rosemary

2 t. dried thyme
2 t. garlic powder
6 to 8 whole peppercorns,
    or 2 t. pepper
6 French rolls, split

Place beef in a 4-quart slow cooker. Combine water, soy sauce and seasonings in a bowl; whisk well and pour over beef. Cover and cook on high setting for 5 to 6 hours, until beef is tender. Remove beef to a plate, reserving broth in slow cooker. Shred beef with a fork; keep warm. Strain broth; skim off any fat and pour into small bowls for dipping. Fill rolls with beef; slice in half and serve. Makes 6 servings.

Slider buns turn any sandwich filling into a bite-size party treat. Just for fun, spear cherry tomatoes and tiny gherkin pickles with a toothpick and use to fasten party sandwiches.

Delicious Diner Burgers

David Wink
Gooseberry Patch

The kids had their hearts set on a cookout in the park, but the weather forecast wasn't promising. So we made these yummy burgers instead. With fries and coleslaw, everybody was happy!

1 onion, sliced	4 cloves garlic, minced
1 stalk celery, chopped	1 T. catsup
2 lbs. lean ground beef	1 t. Italian seasoning
1-1/2 t. salt, divided	1 bay leaf
1/4 t. pepper	6 hamburger buns, split
2 c. tomato juice	

Place onion and celery in a 3-quart slow cooker; set aside. In a large bowl, combine beef, one teaspoon salt and pepper; mix well and shape into 6 patties. Place on top of onion mixture. In a bowl, combine tomato juice, garlic, catsup, Italian seasoning, bay leaf and remaining salt; spoon over patties. Cover and cook on low setting for 7 to 8 hours. Discard bay leaf. Separate patties with a spatula if necessary; serve on buns. Makes 6 servings.

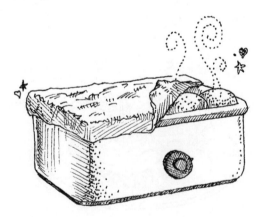

Warm sandwich buns for a crowd...easy! Fill a roaster with buns, cover with heavy-duty aluminum foil and cut several slits in the foil. Top with several dampened paper towels and tightly cover with more foil. Place in a 250-degree oven for 20 minutes, or until rolls are hot and steamy.

Slowly Simmered Flavors
• SLOW COOKER •

Joyce's Sloppy Joes

Lori Mathews-Flannery
Connersville, IN

My co-worker Joyce likes to prepare this for pitch-ins at work.
Everyone always asks for the recipe. Tastes even better the next day!
This beef mixture makes tasty Coney dogs too.

3 lbs. ground beef chuck,
   browned and drained
38-oz. bottle catsup
1/2 c. brown sugar, packed

2 t. garlic powder
1 T. onion powder
12 to 16 sandwich buns, split

Combine all ingredients except buns in a 5-quart slow cooker. Mix well.
Cover and cook on low setting for 2 to 3 hours. To serve, spoon beef
mixture onto buns. Serves 12 to 16.

A fun and simple meal...serve up a chili dog bar! Along with
cooked hot dogs and buns, set out some homemade chili,
shredded cheese, sauerkraut, chopped onions and your
favorite condiments. Kids love it, and it's a terrific way
to use leftover chili.

Southern Pulled Pork Barbecue

Kristin Smith
Bartlesville, OK

Pulled pork is one of my favorite meats on the smoker, but this slow-cooker recipe is just as awesome!

3-lb. boneless pork loin roast, fat trimmed
1 c. water
18-oz. bottle barbecue sauce
2 T. Worcestershire sauce
1 to 2 T. hot pepper sauce

1/4 c. brown sugar, packed
1/2 t. salt
1 t. pepper
8 to 10 hamburger buns, split
Optional: coleslaw

Place roast in a 4-quart slow cooker; add water. Cover and cook on high setting for 7 hours, or until tender. Remove roast to a platter; shred with 2 forks and return to slow cooker. Stir in sauces, brown sugar, salt and pepper; cover and cook on low setting one more hour. Serve pork mixture spooned onto buns and topped with coleslaw, if desired. Makes 8 to 10 servings.

Crocked Pork Butt

Kathy Courington
Canton, GA

I first did this a few years ago and my husband said, "That's a keeper!" It's very simple...add buns and slaw and you're set.

5 to 7-lb. pork butt roast
1 to 2 18-oz. bottles favorite barbecue sauce

sandwich buns, split

Place roast in a 7-quart slow cooker; pour desired amount of sauce over top. Cover and cook on low setting for 8 to 10 hours, until very tender. Shred roast in slow cooker with 2 forks; add more sauce if desired. If less saucy is preferred, uncover for the last hour and turn to high setting to evaporate some of the liquid. To serve, spoon pork mixture onto buns. Serves 9 to 12.

Slowly Simmered Flavors
• SLOW COOKER •

Brats & Sauerkraut

JoAnn
Gooseberry Patch

*Easy game-day food! The recipe is easily doubled, using a
6-quart slow cooker...add just enough beer or apple juice to
cover the brats. Sit back and enjoy the game!*

32-oz. can sauerkraut, drained
1 sweet onion, thinly sliced
5 links bratwurst pork sausage
2 12-oz. cans beer, or
   3 c. apple juice

3 cloves garlic, minced
1 t. salt
1 t. pepper
5 hoagie buns, split
Garnish: choice of mustards

Spread sauerkraut in the bottom of a 4-quart slow cooker; top with
onion slices, then bratwursts. Add beer or apple juice, garlic, salt and
pepper. Cover and cook on high setting for 2 hours. To serve, place
bratwursts on buns; top with mustard and sauerkraut. Makes
5 servings.

A quick & easy side dish...quarter new potatoes and toss
with a little olive oil, salt and pepper. Spread on a baking
sheet and bake at 400 degrees until crisp and golden,
35 to 40 minutes.

Warm Pizza Fondue

Beth Flack
Terre Haute, IN

This fondue is easy to make and stays warm in the slow cooker for serving. It's a favorite of family & friends, especially on Christmas Eve.

2 10-3/4 oz. cans fiesta nacho
   cheese soup
6-oz. pkg. shredded pizza-blend
   cheese
3/4 c. pizza sauce
1/2 c. milk

1/2 c. pepperoni, chopped, or
   mini pepperoni slices
1 t. Italian seasoning
thin wheat crackers or crunchy
   bread sticks

Combine all ingredients except crackers or bread sticks in a 3-quart slow cooker. Cover and cook on low setting for 2 hours, stirring often. Turn slow cooker to warm; serve with crackers or bread sticks. Makes 30 servings.

Hosting a party? Make it easy for guests to mingle and chat... set up food at several tables instead of one big party buffet. Place hot foods on one table, chilled foods at another, sweets at yet another. Your party is sure to be a hit.

Slowly Simmered Flavors
• SLOW COOKER •

White Pizza Dip

Kristy Markners
Fort Mill, SC

*This dip is perfect for snacking while watching the
big game on television!*

16-oz. container sour cream
1 c. ricotta cheese
1 c. shredded mozzarella cheese
2 T. Italian seasoning

2 T. garlic salt or powder
favorite snack crackers or
  tortilla chips

In a 3-quart slow cooker, combine all ingredients except snack crackers
or tortilla chips. Cover and cook on low setting for 2 hours, or until hot
and bubbly. Stir; serve with crackers or chips. Makes 8 to 10 servings.

Pepperoni Dip

Kristin Pittis
Dennison, OH

*I got this recipe from a friend. It's so easy and inexpensive to make
for family get-togethers...and easily doubled for a crowd.*

8-oz. pkg. cream cheese, cubed
10-3/4 oz. can cream of chicken
  soup

5-oz. pkg. pepperoni, chopped
corn chips, tortilla chips or
  pretzels

Combine cream cheese, soup and pepperoni in a 3-quart slow cooker;
stir well. Cover and cook on high setting for 2 to 3 hours, stirring often.
Serve with chips or pretzels. Serves 6.

The secret to being a relaxed hostess...choose foods that
can be prepared in advance. Slow-cooked dips are perfect!

Spicy Chicken Wing Dip

Thomas Smith
Apache Junction, AZ

This delicious dip is fast and easy...you'll love it!

2 8-oz. pkgs. cream cheese,
   softened
1 to 2 5-oz. cans chicken,
   drained and shredded
1 c. hot or mild wing sauce

1/2 c. ranch salad dressing
8-oz. pkg. shredded Cheddar
   cheese
tortilla chips or snack crackers

Spread cream cheese in the bottom of a 3-quart slow cooker. Add chicken, sauce and salad dressing. Top with shredded cheese; mix well. Cover and cook on low setting for 2 hours, or until bubbly and cheese is melted, stirring occasionally. Serve with tortilla chips or crackers. Serves 5 to 8.

Having a party? Freeze your own crystal-clear ice cubes for drinks. Bring a tea kettle of tap water to a boil. Let it cool to room temperature and pour into ice cube trays. Pop ice cubes into a gallon-size plastic freezer bag until party time.

Slowly Simmered Flavors
• SLOW COOKER •

Honey-Garlic Chicken Wings
Nola Coons
Gooseberry Patch

Yum...these wings really get the party started! Use a disposable plastic slow-cooker liner, and you won't need to scrub the crock.

2 to 3 lbs. chicken wings, separated	2 T. soy sauce
1/3 c. honey	2 T. cider vinegar
1/4 c. lemon juice	2 t. garlic powder
1/4 c. water	3/4 t. ground ginger

Add chicken wings to a 4-quart slow cooker; set aside. Whisk together remaining ingredients in a bowl; pour over wings. Stir to mix gently. Cover and cook on low setting for 5 to 6 hours, or on high setting for 3 to 4 hours, until wings are cooked through. Makes 2 to 3 dozen.

Serving yummy-but-sticky finger foods? Fill a mini slow cooker set on low with rolled-up, dampened fingertip towels. Guests will appreciate your thoughtfulness!

151

Spicy Caponata

Carrie O'Shea
Marina Del Rey, CA

This chunky vegetable dip is wonderful and different from the usual party fare. It tastes even better the next day, so it's an easy make-ahead. Any leftovers are delicious with grilled chicken or fish, or spooned into an omelet.

1-1/2 lbs. eggplant, peeled and
    cut into 1/2-inch cubes
1 lb. roma tomatoes, coarsely
    chopped
2 c. zucchini, quartered and
    thinly sliced
1-1/3 c. celery, sliced
1 red or orange pepper, cut into
    1-inch pieces
1 c. sweet onion, chopped
3 T. tomato paste

1 T. sugar
1 t. red pepper flakes
1/2 t. pepper
1/4 c. fresh basil, chopped
1/4 c. fresh parsley, chopped
1/4 c. green olives, drained and
    coarsely chopped
1/4 c. capers, drained and rinsed
2 T. red wine vinegar
toasted baguette slices or
    assorted crackers

Spray a 5-quart slow cooker with non-stick vegetable spray. Combine vegetables, tomato paste, sugar and seasonings in slow cooker; mix well. Cover and cook on low setting for 4 to 5 hours, until vegetables are tender. Remove crock from slow cooker. Stir in herbs, olives, capers and vinegar; allow to cool completely. Cover and refrigerate until chilled. Serve with baguettes or crackers, chilled or at room temperature. Makes about 8 cups.

Dips are twice as tasty with homemade baguette crisps.
Thinly slice a French loaf and arrange slices on a baking sheet.
Sprinkle with olive oil and garlic powder, then bake at
400 degrees for 12 to 15 minutes, until golden.

Slowly Simmered Flavors
• SLOW COOKER •

Warm Chicken Nacho Dip

Vickie
Gooseberry Patch

You'll want to serve this scrumptious dip with scoop-type tortilla chips, to get every bite!

16-oz. pkg. pasteurized process
   cheese, cubed
14-oz. can diced tomatoes with
   green chiles, drained
2 boneless, skinless chicken
   breasts, cooked and shredded
1/3 c. sour cream

1/4 c. green onions, diced
1-1/2 T. taco seasoning mix
Optional: 2 T. jalapeño pepper,
   minced
1 c. black beans, drained
   and rinsed
optional: small amount milk

In a 4-quart slow cooker, combine all ingredients except beans and milk; mix well. Cover and cook on high setting for one to 2 hours, stirring occasionally, until bubbly and cheese has melted. Stir in beans; if consistency is too thick, stir in a little milk. Cover and cook another 15 minutes, or until heated through. Makes 12 servings.

Mix up your own taco seasoning. In a jar, combine 3/4 cup dried, minced onion, 1/4 cup each salt and chili powder, 2 tablespoons each cornstarch, red pepper flakes, ground cumin and dried, minced garlic and one tablespoon dried oregano. Four tablespoons of the mix equals a 1-1/4 ounce envelope.

Taco Joe Dip

Kim Wallace
Dennison, OH

Such a versatile recipe! This is a great party dip. You can also turn it into a meal...stir in some cooked rice and spoon into flour tortillas to make burritos. You can even turn it into soup by adding a 29-ounce can of tomato sauce to the slow cooker. Enjoy!

1 lb. ground beef
1-1/4 oz. pkg. taco seasoning
   mix
14-1/2 oz. can stewed tomatoes
16-oz. can kidney beans, rinsed
   and drained
15-oz. can black beans, rinsed
   and drained
15-1/4 oz. can corn, drained

4-oz. can chopped green chiles,
   drained
8-oz. can tomato sauce
1 c. onion, diced
1/2 c. green pepper, chopped
8-oz. pkg. shredded Cheddar
   cheese
tortilla chips

Brown beef in a skillet over medium heat. Drain; stir in taco seasoning and transfer to a 5-quart slow cooker. Add tomatoes with juice, beans, corn, chiles, tomato sauce, onion and green pepper; mix well. Cover and cook on low setting for 5 to 7 hours, until hot and bubbly. At serving time, stir in shredded cheese. Serve with tortilla chips. Serves 6 to 8.

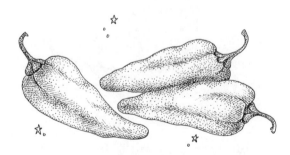

Some like it hot...try using extra-spicy chiles and Mexican-blend cheese in your Taco Joe Dip for extra zing!

Slowly Simmered Flavors
• SLOW COOKER •

Teriyaki Meatballs

Lori Mulhern
Rosemount, MN

These meatballs are very good...a nice change from BBQ meatballs.
They're always popular on my holiday appetizer buffets.

80 frozen meatballs	1/2 c. soy sauce
1 c. unsweetened pineapple juice	1-1/2 c. sugar
1 c. water	1/4 c. cornstarch
1 c. white vinegar	

Bake meatballs according to package directions. Transfer to a 4-quart slow cooker and set aside. Meanwhile, combine remaining ingredients in a saucepan. Cook and stir over medium heat until mixture comes to a boil and sugar dissolves. Pour mixture over meatballs in slow cooker. Turn to warm setting for serving. Serves 15 to 20.

Platters of food set on different levels make a more interesting party presentation. Use a stack of plates or upside-down pots and bowls on a buffet table to create different heights, cover with a tablecloth and set serving dishes on top!

Caramel Apple Crumble

Cassie Hooker
La Porte, TX

I love to make this in the fall and winter months. It's a great warm treat to enjoy while sitting by the cozy fireplace.

5 apples, peeled, cored and cut into chunks
1-2/3 c. brown sugar, packed and divided
1/2 c. sugar
1/4 t. salt

1-1/2 t. cinnamon, divided
2/3 c. quick-cooking oats, uncooked
1/4 c. all-purpose flour
3 to 4 T. butter, softened
1 t. vanilla extract

In a bowl, combine apples, one cup brown sugar, sugar, salt and one teaspoon cinnamon. Spread evenly in a 5-quart slow cooker. In another bowl, combine remaining brown sugar, remaining cinnamon and other ingredients; mix until crumbly. Sprinkle crumb mixture over apple mixture. Cover and cook on low setting for 4 hours, or on high setting for 2 hours, until apples are tender. Remove crock from slow cooker. Let stand, covered, for one hour to allow the caramel to thicken. Serve warm. Serves 6 to 8.

Spoon generous portions of a warm, gooey dessert
into stemmed glasses and dollop with whipped topping...
a sweet ending that your guests will long remember!

Nutty Pumpkin Pie Pudding
Mel Chencharick
Julian, PA

This delicious recipe is almost like a dump cake, only it's pudding and it's made in a slow cooker...we love it!

15-oz. can pumpkin
5-oz. can evaporated milk
1/3 c. sugar
2 T. pumpkin pie spice, divided
9-oz. pkg. yellow cake mix

1 c. pecans or walnuts, toasted
and chopped
1/4 c. butter, melted
Garnish: whipped topping

Lightly coat a 4-quart slow cooker with non-stick vegetable spray. Add pumpkin, evaporated milk, sugar and one tablespoon spice. Stir well; spread evenly in slow cooker and set aside. In a bowl, stir together dry cake mix, nuts and remaining spice. Sprinkle evenly over pumpkin mixture. Drizzle melted butter over all. Cover and cook on high setting for 2-1/2 hours. Remove crock from slow cooker; uncover and allow to cool for 30 minutes. To serve, spoon warm pudding into dessert dishes; add a dollop of whipped topping. Makes 4 to 6 servings.

The long, sweet hours that
bring us all things good.
– Alfred, Lord Tennyson

Warm Peach Crisp

Marsha Baker
Pioneer, OH

I was so pleased the first time I made this delectable dessert!
It has become a family favorite. Add a scoop of cinnamon
ice cream...yummy!

2 15-oz. cans sliced peaches,
   well drained
3/4 c. brown sugar, packed
1 c. quick-cooking oats,
   uncooked

1/2 c. all-purpose flour
1 t. cinnamon
Optional: freshly grated nutmeg
   to taste
1/4 c. butter, softened

Spray a 3-quart slow cooker with non-stick vegetable spray. Add peaches and set aside. In a bowl, stir together brown sugar, oats, flour, cinnamon and nutmeg, if using. Cut in butter with a pastry blender or 2 forks until mixture is crumbly. Stir half of crumb mixture into peaches; spread remaining crumbs on top. Place 2 paper towels on top of crock. Cover and cook on low setting for 3 to 4 hours, checking for doneness after 3 hours. Serve warm. Makes 5 to 6 servings.

Dollop fresh whipped cream on warm slow-cooker desserts... irresistible! Pour a pint of whipping cream into a deep, narrow bowl. Beat with an electric mixer on medium speed, gradually increasing to high speed, until soft peaks form. Add sugar and vanilla to taste.

Custard Rice Pudding

Janis Parr
Ontario, Canada

This custard-like rice pudding is comfort food at its best. Cooking it in a slow cooker makes it smooth and creamy and oh-so good.

2-1/2 c. cooked white rice
1-1/2 c. milk
2/3 c. sugar
3 eggs, beaten
3 T. butter, melted

2 t. vanilla extract
1/2 t. cinnamon
1/4 t. ground nutmeg
1/2 c. raisins
Garnish: whipped cream

Combine all ingredients except garnish in a bowl; mix well. Pour into a greased 4-quart slow cooker. Cover and cook on low setting for 4 to 6 hours, or on high setting for one to 2 hours. Stir once during the last 30 minutes. Serve warm, topped with whipped cream. Makes 6 servings.

If you love to bake, keep a small vintage nutmeg grater on hand for grating whole nutmegs. The extra-fresh flavor can't be beat.

Hot Fudge Spoon Cake

Jen Licon-Conner
Gooseberry Patch

This pudding-like dessert has a layer of chocolate cake with a gooey hot fudge layer underneath! Perfect any time of year, but especially good on a chilly winter night.

1 c. all-purpose flour
7 T. baking cocoa, divided
2 t. baking powder
1/4 t. salt
1-3/4 c. light brown sugar, divided

1/2 c. milk
2 T. butter, melted
1/2 t. vanilla extract
1-3/4 c. hot water
Garnish: vanilla ice cream

Into a large bowl, sift flour, 3 tablespoons baking cocoa, baking powder, salt and one cup brown sugar, rubbing the brown sugar through sifter to remove any lumps. Mix well; whisk in milk, melted butter and vanilla. Spread batter evenly in a lightly greased 4-quart slow cooker. Mix together remaining brown sugar and remaining baking cocoa; sprinkle evenly over batter. Pour hot water over all; do not stir. Cover and cook on high setting for 2 hours, or until a toothpick inserted one-inch deep in center tests clean. To serve, spoon warm cake into dessert bowls; top with a scoop of ice cream. Makes 6 servings.

Take along a dessert in a slow cooker to a party or meeting... simply wrap it in a towel to keep it warm. Serve within an hour or plug it in at a low setting. You're sure to be everybody's new best friend!

Handy
Kitchen
Helpers

Chicken Tetrazzini

Laura Tressler
Mount Joy, PA

An old comfort-food favorite...so easy to make in the microwave!

8-oz. pkg. spaghetti, uncooked
6 T. butter, melted and divided
1/4 c. all-purpose flour
1/2 t. Italian seasoning
1/2 t. salt
1/4 t. pepper

1 c. chicken broth
1 c. evaporated milk
2 c. cooked chicken, cubed or
shredded
1/4 c. grated Parmesan cheese
1/4 c. soft bread crumbs

Cook spaghetti according to package directions; drain. Meanwhile, in a microwave-safe glass casserole dish, combine 1/4 cup melted butter, flour, seasonings, broth and milk. Mix well. Microwave, uncovered, on medium-high setting for 8 to 9 minutes, stirring every 2 minutes. Add cooked spaghetti, chicken and Parmesan cheese; stir together. Cover and microwave on medium-high setting for 5 to 6 minutes, stirring after 3 minutes. Toss together bread crumbs and remaining butter; sprinkle over top. Microwave, uncovered, 2 minutes more. Serves 4.

Buying boneless, skinless chicken breasts in bulk? Cook them all at once. Season with salt and pepper, if desired, and allow to cool. Pack in freezer bags in recipe-size portions. Kept in the freezer, they'll be ready for quick lunches, sandwiches and all kinds of dinners!

Handy Kitchen Helpers
• MICROWAVE •

Mom's BBQ Chicken

Ronda Branneman
Jeffersonville, IN

*This is the best sauce...not too spicy like some! Everyone will
love it...and no need to light the grill.*

1 c. catsup	1 t. paprika
2 T. vinegar	1/4 t. salt
2 T. onion, finely chopped	pepper to taste
1 T. brown sugar, packed	2 to 3 lbs. chicken drumsticks
1 T. Worcestershire sauce	or leg quarters
1 t. sugar	1/4 c. butter, melted

Combine all ingredients except chicken and butter in a microwave-safe
one-quart bowl; mix well. Microwave, uncovered, on high setting for
5 minutes. Stir after 3 minutes, or when sauce is hot and thick enough
to coat a spoon. Arrange chicken in a microwave-safe glass baking pan.
Brush chicken with butter; spoon sauce over chicken. Cover with
microwave-safe plastic wrap. Microwave on high setting for 25 to
30 minutes, until chicken juices run clear when pierced. Let stand,
covered, for 5 minutes before serving. Makes 4 to 6 servings.

It's a snap to steam fresh vegetables in the microwave.
Place sliced veggies in a microwave-safe dish and add
a little water. Cover with plastic wrap and vent with a knife
tip. Microwave on high for 2 to 5 minutes, checking after
each minute, until crisp-tender. Uncover carefully to
let hot steam escape.

Quick Steak & Veggies

Linda Scarborough
Mechanicsville, VA

My original recipe for a satisfying one-dish dinner.
Serve with toasted French bread.

2 T. butter, divided
1 lb. beef cube steak, cut into
    4 to 6 pieces
1/2 c. instant-cooking rice,
    uncooked

1/2 c. water
1/4 t. salt
14-1/2 oz. cans peas & carrots
7-oz. can sliced mushrooms
pepper to taste

Melt one tablespoon butter in a heavy skillet over medium-high heat.
Add steak; brown on both sizes. Remove to a plate and cool; cut into
bite-size pieces. Meanwhile, in a microwave-safe casserole dish, stir
together uncooked rice, water, salt and remaining butter. Cover and
microwave on high setting for 3 minutes; remove from microwave and
let stand for 5 minutes. Transfer rice to a bowl; fluff with a fork and set
aside. To the same casserole dish, add undrained peas & carrots and
mushrooms. Microwave on high setting for about 3 minutes. Add
vegetable mixture and steak to rice; toss to mix. Season with pepper
and serve. Serves 4 to 6.

Roasted garlic is delicious spread on fresh bread and so
easy in the microwave! Slice the top off a whole garlic bulb
and set in a microwave-safe container. Season to taste with
olive oil, salt and pepper, sprinkle with water and cover
with plastic wrap. Microwave on high setting for 8 minutes,
until soft. To use, simply squeeze out the soft garlic.

Micro Stuffed Peppers

Sharon Haddock
Klamath Falls, OR

I have been making this recipe ever since I received my first microwave oven in 1976. Believe me, this is a "tried & true" recipe that I go to month after month, season after season! Use ground turkey instead of beef, if you prefer.

2 green peppers	1/8 t. pepper
3/4 lb. ground beef	10-3/4 oz. can tomato soup,
1 c. cooked rice	divided
2 T. dried, minced onion	1/2 c. water
3/4 t. garlic, minced	4 slices sharp Cheddar cheese
3/4 t. salt	

Cut off tops of green peppers; remove seeds and ribs. Cut peppers in half and place in a microwave-safe casserole dish. In a bowl, mix uncooked beef with rice, onion, garlic and seasonings. Add 1/3 of soup to beef mixture and mix well. Fill pepper halves with beef mixture. In a separate bowl, whisk water into remaining soup; spoon over and around peppers. Cover and microwave on high setting for 18 to 22 minutes. Top each pepper with a slice of cheese, overlapping slices. Cover again and microwave for one to 2 minutes, until cheese melts. Serve peppers topped with the sauce that forms in the bottom of the dish. Serves 4.

If your children don't like green peppers, give red, yellow and orange peppers a try. The milder taste may just win them over.

Almost-Instant Cowboy Chicken

Kelly Gray
Avon Park, FL

As a busy preschool teacher, this chicken dish is a real favorite of mine since it can be whipped up in ten minutes. I named it Cowboy Chicken because it looks like an ample Western-inspired dish. If you have "big boy eaters" in your home, this is a sure-fire way to fill them up, without leaving you with a sink full of dirty dishes.

22-oz. pkg. frozen grilled chicken breasts, thawed
2 T. oil
2 T. butter
1 onion, sliced
1 t. garlic salt
1/2 t. pepper
1-1/2 c. shredded Monterey Jack cheese, divided
16 slices pre-cooked bacon
barbecue sauce to taste
Optional: cooked, buttered egg noodles

Spray a skillet with non-stick vegetable spray. Add chicken and cook for 4 minutes per side, just until golden. Transfer to a microwave-safe plate; set aside. Heat oil and butter in skillet. Add onion; cook until translucent and edges are golden. Sprinkle with seasonings; set aside. Sprinkle chicken with a thin layer of cheese; top each piece with 2 slices bacon and remaining cheese. Microwave, uncovered, on high setting for 2 minutes, or until chicken is heated through and cheese is melted. Spoon onion mixture over chicken; drizzle with barbecue sauce. If desired, serve chicken over buttered egg noodles. Makes 8 servings.

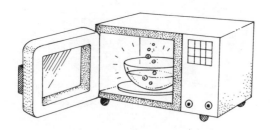

For a citrusy fresh, clean microwave, fill a microwave-safe cup with one cup water and 1/4 cup lemon juice. Heat on high for 3 minutes, then wipe down the inside of the microwave using a soft damp cloth.

Handy Kitchen Helpers
• MICROWAVE •

Jen's Chicken & Green Bean Casserole

Jennifer McIntosh
Fillmore, CA

*Topped with mashed potatoes, this dish is like a shepherd's pie.
If you want to make eight servings, just add another
can of green beans and another 1/3 cup of milk.*

6 servings instant mashed
  potatoes
10-3/4 oz. can cream of
  mushroom soup
1/4 c. milk

1 c. shredded Cheddar cheese
2 c. cooked chicken, cubed
14-1/2 oz. can cut green beans,
  drained
Garnish: French fried onions

Prepare potatoes according to package directions; set aside. In a large
microwave-safe casserole dish, whisk together soup, milk and cheese;
fold in chicken and beans. Microwave, loosely covered, on high setting
for 5 minutes, or until heated through. Spoon mashed potatoes over
mixture; top with onions. Microwave for another 5 more minutes, or
until onions are browned. Makes 6 servings.

Zippy & Zesty Baked Beans

Pam Massey
Marshall, AR

*A simple side dish that's really good! For variety, stir in
some leftover ground beef. Serve with cornbread.*

5 to 6 slices bacon, chopped
1/4 c. to 1/2 c. onion, chopped
2 15-oz. cans pork & beans

8-oz. can zesty tomato sauce
  with green chiles
1/4 c. brown sugar, packed

Add bacon and onion to a microwave-safe glass bowl. Cover and
microwave on high setting until bacon is nearly done, but not too crisp.
Drain most of the drippings; stir in remaining ingredients. Cover and
microwave for 8 to 10 minutes, stirring once or twice. Let stand for
10 minutes before serving. Makes 8 servings.

Mexican Meatloaf

Gretchen Bouliane
Dorchester Center, MA

My husband likes meat loaf...I don't. I love Mexican food...
he doesn't. This is a compromise that we both can live with,
and it's quick & easy to make. Nice with Spanish rice!

1 lb. ground chicken
1/2 c. soft bread crumbs
1 egg, beaten
1 t. ground cumin

1/2 t. ground coriander
1 c. favorite salsa, divided
1/2 c. shredded Mexican-blend
   cheese

In a large bowl, combine chicken, bread crumbs, egg, seasonings and
1/2 cup salsa; mix until well blended. Transfer to a small microwave-
safe loaf pan coated with non-stick vegetable spray. Cover with plastic
wrap; microwave on high setting for 5 minutes. Sprinkle with cheese;
top with remaining salsa and microwave for 5 more minutes. Let stand
in microwave for 2 minutes; slice and serve. Serves 4 to 6.

Twice-Baked Potatoes

Judi Towner
West End, NC

This is a fun recipe for a delicious side dish. My teenage daughter
loved making these twice-baked potatoes...they look as if you went
to a lot more trouble to make them. Guests rave about them!

4 baking potatoes
1/2 c. butter, softened
1/2 c. sour cream

1/2 t. salt
1/8 t. pepper
paprika to taste

Pierce potatoes with a fork. Place a paper towel on microwave carousel
plate; arrange potatoes in a circle, one inch apart. Microwave on high
setting for 12 to 16 minutes; let stand to soften and cool. Slice tops off
potatoes; scoop out centers into a bowl. Add butter, sour cream, salt and
pepper. Mix well with an electric mixer on low speed until smooth.
Spoon potato mixture into potato shells; microwave on high setting for
4 minutes. Sprinkle lightly with paprika; serve immediately. Serves 4.

Handy Kitchen Helpers
• MICROWAVE •

Barbecued Meatballs

Kim Wallace
Dennison, OH

My family loves these meatballs! I serve them with rice or potatoes and veggies, or sometimes as meatball sandwiches. I have even made hamburger patties out of this mixture for barbecued hamburgers. What's really nice about this recipe...you make it in the microwave!

2 lbs. ground beef
2/3 c. soft bread crumbs
3/4 c. onion, finely chopped
1/2 c. milk
1 T. prepared horseradish
1/4 t. garlic salt
1/4 t. seasoned salt

1/4 t. pepper
6 to 8 thin slices onion
1-1/2 c. catsup
2 T. vinegar
2 T. honey
4 t. Worcestershire sauce

In a large bowl, combine beef, bread crumbs, chopped onion, milk, horseradish and seasonings. Mix well; form into 2-inch meatballs. Place meatballs in a microwave-safe dish; arrange onion slices on top. Cover and microwave on high setting for 6 to 8 minutes, until no longer pink inside. In a separate bowl, stir together remaining ingredients; spoon over meatballs. Cover and microwave on high for an additional 5 to 8 minutes, until heated through. Serves 6 to 8.

This 5-minute cheese dip can't be beat. Cut a pound of pasteurized process cheese into cubes and place in a microwave-safe dish. Pour a can of diced tomatoes with green chiles over top. Microwave on high setting for 5 minutes, stirring after 3 minutes.

Zucchini & Stuffing Bake

Marjorie Wright
Coshocton, OH

A tasty recipe to use up all those garden zucchini! My husband and I enjoy the first dish, and my daughter living next door gets the second dish.

7 c. zucchini, peeled and diced
2 carrots, peeled and finely
   chopped
1 green pepper, diced
3/4 c. onion, diced
8-oz. container sour cream
10-3/4 oz. can cream of
   chicken soup
6-oz. pkg. chicken-flavored
   stuffing mix
1/2 c. margarine, melted
Garnish: dry bread crumbs,
   dried parsley, paprika

Combine all vegetables in a microwave-safe glass bowl. Cover with plastic wrap; microwave on high setting for 15 minutes. Let stand for 5 minutes; drain. In a separate bowl, combine sour cream and soup; toss stuffing mix with margarine and stir in. Blend soup mixture with vegetables. Divide between 2 microwave-safe casserole dishes; garnish as desired. Cover and microwave each dish on high for 8 to 9 minutes. Makes 2 dishes, 4 to 6 servings per dish.

Bessie's Hot Corn

Christy Bonner
Bessemer, AL

One of my husband's great-aunts shared this recipe with me.

2 15-oz. cans corn, drained
2 8-oz. pkgs. cream cheese,
   cubed
3 to 4 jalapeño peppers, chopped
2 to 3 dashes hot pepper sauce
8-oz. pkg. shredded sharp
   Cheddar cheese, divided

Combine corn and cream cheese in a microwave-safe 2-quart casserole dish. Microwave, uncovered, on high setting for 5 minutes, stirring occasionally, until cream cheese and corn mix easily. Stir in jalapeños, hot sauce and one cup shredded cheese. Top with remaining shredded cheese. Microwave for an additional 3 minutes. Serves 8.

Cauliflower Gratin

Liz Plotnick-Snay
Gooseberry Patch

Whenever I serve this dish, everyone happily eats their vegetables!

1 lb. cauliflower flowerets
1 lb. broccoli flowerets
1/2 c. water
1/2 c. cream cheese, cubed
1/4 c. milk
1/2 c. sour cream

1-1/2 c. shredded sharp Cheddar
  cheese
10 round buttery crackers,
  crushed
3 T. grated Parmesan cheese

Combine vegetables in a microwave-safe 2-quart casserole dish; add
water. Cover and microwave on high setting for 8 to 10 minutes, until
tender; drain. Combine cream cheese and milk in a microwave-safe
2-cup measuring cup; microwave for one minute and stir well. Stir in
sour cream; spoon over vegetables. Sprinkle Cheddar cheese over top.
Microwave for 2 minutes, or until cheese is melted. Combine cracker
crumbs and Parmesan cheese; sprinkle over vegetables and serve.
Serves 8.

Zucchini Casserole

Tana Simcox
Sandoval, IL

*My great-grandmother and I used to make this casserole together
at least twice a week when I was a little girl.*

4 slices bacon
1/4 c. onion, chopped
2 to 3 zucchini, sliced

1 c. pizza sauce
8-oz. pkg. shredded mozzarella
  cheese

Place bacon in a microwave-safe casserole dish. Microwave on high
for 3 to 4 minutes, until crisp. Drain on a paper towel. Add onion to
drippings in dish; microwave, uncovered, for 3 to 4 minutes. Add
zucchini, pizza sauce and crumbled bacon; stir to coat with sauce. Cover
and microwave for 10 to 15 minutes. Top with cheese; microwave for
2 to 3 minutes, until cheese is melted. Cool slightly. Serves 4.

Meatless Minestrone Soup

JoAnn
Gooseberry Patch

Quick to make in the microwave! Just add a basket of warm
Italian bread for a great lunch or light dinner.

2 carrots, peeled, halved and
  thinly sliced
1 red pepper, diced
1/2 lb. green beans, trimmed
  and cut into 2-inch lengths
3 cloves garlic, minced
2 t. olive oil
15-1/2 oz. can navy beans,
  drained and rinsed

14-1/2 oz. can chicken broth
1 c. water
1/3 c. couscous, rinsed and
  uncooked
2 T. tomato paste
1/2 t. salt
1 to 2 T. fresh parsley, chopped
Garnish: shredded Parmesan
  cheese

In a microwave-safe 3-quart dish, combine vegetables, garlic and oil;
stir. Cover and microwave on high for 5 minutes. Stir in remaining
ingredients except parsley and cheese. Cover and microwave on high for
about 5 minutes, until vegetables and couscous are tender. Stir in
parsley; garnish with cheese. Serves 4.

For an easy beginning to a savory meal, sprinkle a little dish
of extra virgin olive oil lightly with Parmesan cheese, Italian
seasoning and salt. Set out with a piping-hot loaf
of crusty bread for dipping.

Handy Kitchen Helpers
• MICROWAVE •

Broccoli-Cheese Soup

Helen Cannon
Hope Mills, NC

Soup from the microwave! This is quick & easy but so delicious.

2 10-oz. pkgs. frozen chopped
   broccoli
3/4 c. onion, chopped
2 T. oil
6 c. chicken broth
1/8 t. garlic powder

Optional: 1 t. salt
8-oz. pkg. medium egg noodles,
   uncooked
2 c. milk
16-oz. pkg. pasteurized process
   cheese, shredded

Microwave broccoli according to package directions; drain and set aside.
In a large microwave-safe bowl, combine onion and oil; stir to mix.
Microwave, uncovered, on high setting for 2 to 3 minutes, until onion
is tender. Add broth; microwave for 3 minutes. Stir in seasonings and
uncooked noodles; microwave for 3 minutes. Add broccoli to soup;
microwave for 4 minutes. Stir in milk and cheese; microwave just until
cheese is melted. Stir again before serving. Serves 6.

Bouillon cubes are an easy substitute for canned chicken
and beef broth. To make one cup of broth, dissolve a bouillon
cube in one cup of boiling water. Use 1-3/4 cups prepared
bouillon to replace a 14-ounce can of broth.

173

Quick Apple Crisp

Ginger Miller
Seven Valleys, PA

My husband loves apple pie, and when I am in a hurry, I can make this in a jiffy! If the granola is omitted, it can be served as a tasty side dish for roast pork or baked ham.

1/4 c. butter
1/3 c. sugar
1/4 t. cinnamon
1/4 t. nutmeg
1/8 t. salt
1 t. tapioca, uncooked

3 to 4 cooking apples, peeled, cored and sliced
Optional: 1/2 c. raisins
1/2 c. granola
Garnish: whipped cream or ice cream

Melt butter in a microwave-safe 8"x8" glass baking pan. In a cup, combine sugar, spices and tapioca; stir into butter. Add apples and raisins, if using; toss to coat evenly. Microwave, uncovered, on high setting for 5 to 6 minutes, until apples are tender. Top with granola. Serve warm, topped with whipped cream or ice cream. Serves 4.

Micro Pineapple Upside-Down Cake

Joan Chance
Houston, TX

This recipe has won me many prizes! It can be adapted for other fruits as well.

1/4 c. butter
1/2 c. brown sugar, packed
6 slices canned pineapple
6 maraschino cherries

9-oz. pkg. yellow cake mix
Garnish: ice cream or whipped topping

Melt butter in a microwave-safe 9" round glass baking pan. Stir in brown sugar. Arrange pineapple slices in pan; place a cherry in the center of each. Mix cake batter as directed on package; pour batter over pineapple slices. Microwave, uncovered, on medium-high setting for 7 minutes. Microwave on high setting for 2 to 4 minutes, until a toothpick tests clean. Let stand one minute; invert cake onto a serving plate. Garnish as desired. Makes 8 servings.

Quick Black Forest Cake Dessert

Wendy Ball
Battle Creek, MI

During the summer, who wants to heat up the kitchen, even for dessert? This is a great way to get your kids or grandkids interested in baking and helping in the kitchen!

9-oz. pkg. chocolate cake mix
1 egg, beaten
1/3 c. oil
1/2 c. water

21-oz. can cherry pie filling
Garnish: whipped topping
Optional: chocolate shavings or
    mini chocolate chips

In a bowl, combine dry cake mix, egg, oil and water. Beat for 2 minutes; pour batter into a greased microwave-safe straight-sided 8" or 9" baking pan. Microwave on high setting for 5 to 6 minutes. Cake will not brown, but is done when no longer wet on top and sides pull away a little from the pan. Let stand one minute; invert cake onto a serving plate and allow to cool. Drizzle pie filling over the top, letting it run down the sides. Top with whipped topping. If desired, garnish with chocolate shavings or chips. Makes 4 to 6 servings.

Chocolate shavings look so delicate, yet are really simple to make. Just pull a vegetable peeler across a bar of chocolate and watch it curl!

Muddy Chicken Skewers & Coleslaw

Nichole Sullivan
Santa Fe, TX

The name may be surprising, but let me tell you, these are so tasty! I call this "Muddy Chicken" because the balsamic in the marinade gives it that mud color. But don't let that fool you...it's delicious. This is such an easy, simple & low-calorie recipe.

2/3 c. balsamic vinegar
2/3 c. Dijon mustard
1/2 c. olive oil
1/2 T. garlic, minced
1 T. honey

kosher salt and pepper to taste
1 lb. boneless, skinless chicken
    breasts, cut into large cubes
4 to 6 wooden skewers

In a large bowl, combine all ingredients except chicken; whisk to blend well. Use 1/2 cup of marinade to prepare Coleslaw. Add cubed chicken to remaining marinade and toss gently, coating each piece. Cover and refrigerate for 30 minutes to one hour. Drain chicken, discarding marinade; thread chicken onto skewers. Grill on a countertop or panini grill on high setting for 12 to 15 minutes, turning often, until chicken is cooked through and juices run clear. Serve with Coleslaw. Serves 4 to 6.

Coleslaw:

1 c. carrots, peeled
1/2 onion, peeled

1/2 head cabbage, cored
1/2 c. reserved marinade

In a food processor, shred carrots, onion and cabbage; combine in a bowl. Pour reserved marinade over mixture; and stir to blend well. Chill before serving.

Soak wooden skewers in water at least 20 minutes before using...they won't burn or stick.

Herbed Pork Chops

Robin Hill
Rochester, NY

My husband and I love the flavor of these grilled chops.

1/4 t. dried thyme	4 5-oz. boneless pork loin chops,
1/4 t. paprika	1/2-inch thick
1/4 t. dry mustard	2 t. soy sauce
1/4 t. salt	1/2 t. sugar
1/4 t. pepper	

Combine seasonings in a cup; rub mixture over both sides of pork chops. Combine soy sauce and sugar; brush over tops only of pork chops. Let stand for 20 minutes. Arrange pork chops on a preheated countertop grill set to high. Grill for 4 to 5 minutes, until golden and no longer pink in the center. Makes 4 servings.

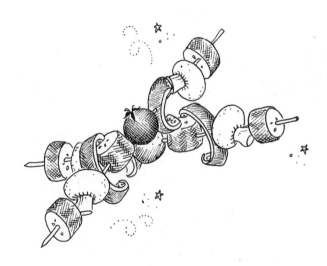

Grill some veggies alongside your pork chops. Asparagus spears, thinly sliced zucchini and wedges of red pepper are some good choices. Brush lightly with olive oil, season with salt & pepper and place on grill...they'll cook in about the same amount of time as the chops.

GG's Grilled Cheese

Julie Dossantos
Fort Pierce, FL

One of my favorite things to make on the grill is grilled cheese sandwiches. My grandmother loved grilled cheese with tomato... this recipe was created with her in mind! She gave my husband and me a George Foreman Grill when we were married, and we use it often. Yummy!

1 T. mayonnaise
2 slices whole-wheat or
   ciabatta bread
2 slices Swiss cheese
1/2 roma tomato, thinly sliced
   and divided

1/2 avocado, peeled, pitted,
   thinly sliced and divided
Optional: salt to taste

Spread mayonnaise over one side of both bread slices. Place one slice, mayonnaise-side down, on a countertop grill. Top with one slice cheese and half each of tomato and avocado. Season vegetables with a little salt, if desired. Top with remaining slices of cheese and bread. Close grill; press down on sandwich. Cook on high setting for about 2 to 3 minutes. Remove to a plate. Let stand for one to 2 minutes; cut in half. Serve with remaining tomato and avocado slices. Makes one sandwich.

Grilled cheese and tomato soup...is there anything more comforting? For delicious soup in a jiffy, heat together a can of condensed tomato soup and a can of diced tomatoes until hot. Stir in a little cream...yum!

Handy Kitchen Helpers
• COUNTERTOP GRILL •

Italian Pepperoni Panini

Angela Davis
Guilford, IN

One day, my husband took some leftovers and made an excellent sandwich. This recipe is my attempt to recreate the sandwich.

2 thin slices French bread
1 T. shredded Parmesan cheese
5 slices pepperoni

2 slices deli ham
2 T. shredded mozzarella cheese
softened butter to taste

Sprinkle one bread slice with Parmesan cheese. Add pepperoni and ham; sprinkle with mozzarella cheese and top with remaining bread slice. Spread butter lightly over the outside of sandwich. Place on a countertop or panini grill; cook on high setting until golden and cheese is melted. Makes one sandwich.

Panini George Sandwich

Jamie Pennington
Princeton, IL

Delicious! Try it with thinly sliced grilled chicken breast instead of the roast beef, too.

1 green pepper, thinly sliced
1 red pepper, thinly sliced
1 onion, thinly sliced
2 to 3 t. olive oil
1 lb. deli roast beef, shredded

12 thick slices favorite bread
sweet & spicy mustard to taste
6 to 12 slices Pepper Jack or
   Cheddar cheese

In a skillet over medium heat, sauté peppers and onion in oil. Add beef; heat through. Spread one side of bread slices with mustard. Layer cheese, pepper mixture and beef on 6 slices of bread; close sandwiches. Lightly grease a countertop grill set on high; add sandwiches and cook until toasted and cheese is melted. Serves 6.

The best way to cheer yourself up
is to cheer someone else up.

– Mark Twain

Polynesian Steaks & Smashed Potatoes

Cheri Maxwell
Gulf Breeze, FL

There's no need to go out to celebrate! Just add a salad tossed with gingered dressing and pineapple sherbet for dessert. Enjoy!

1/4 c. soy sauce	2 cloves garlic, minced
2 t. honey	2 6-oz. beef sirloin steaks

Combine soy sauce, honey and garlic. Brush half of marinade over both sides of steaks; cover and refrigerate for one hour. Meanwhile, cook potatoes for Smashed Potatoes; set aside. Grill steaks on a preheated countertop or panini grill for 3 minutes. Brush remaining marinade over tops of steaks. Grill for one more minute, or to desired doneness. Set aside steaks; keep warm while grilling Smashed Potatoes. Serve steaks with potatoes. Serves 2.

Smashed Potatoes:

1/2 lb. new redskin potatoes	3/4 t. dried rosemary
1 T. olive oil	salt and pepper to taste

Cover potatoes with water in a saucepan. Cook over medium-high heat until fork-tender, 15 to 20 minutes; drain. Place hot potatoes on a cutting board; press flat with a potato masher, forming round discs. Drizzle with oil; sprinkle with seasonings. Arrange potatoes on countertop grill set on high. Cook until crisp and golden, 4 to 6 minutes.

Don't have a countertop grill? Steak and chop recipes can be prepared using an oven broiler or a stovetop ridged grill pan. Give it a try!

Handy Kitchen Helpers
• COUNTERTOP GRILL •

Vince's Fiesta Chicken

Darci Heaton
Woodbury, PA

After a long day at work, and being seven months pregnant, I came home to find this meal as a surprise from my husband. It was so good, and I was so impressed that he came up with it on his own, without a recipe!

3 boneless, skinless chicken
   breasts, pounded thin
1 c. Italian salad dressing

5.6-oz. pkg. Spanish rice mix
3 slices sharp Cheddar cheese
1 c. corn & black bean salsa

Place chicken in a large plastic zipping bag. Add salad dressing; close bag and refrigerate for 2 to 3 hours. Prepare rice according to package directions. Meanwhile, remove chicken from bag and allow excess dressing to drain. Discard bag and remaining dressing. Grill chicken on a countertop grill set on high for 5 to 6 minutes, until no longer pink and juices run clear. Top each piece with a cheese slice; let stand until melted. To serve, divide rice among 3 dinner plates; top each with a piece of chicken and 1/3 cup salsa. Serve immediately. Makes 3 servings.

Flattened boneless chicken breasts cook up quickly and evenly. Simply place chicken between two pieces of plastic wrap and gently pound to desired thickness with a meat mallet or a small skillet.

Fiber & Protein Onion Burgers

Louise Graybiel
Toronto, Ontario

I came up with these after my husband and I were both told by our doctors to lower our cholesterol. We wanted the meaty taste of a "real" burger, but without the saturated fat. They're budget-friendly too... because they're much leaner than traditional burgers, the patties don't shrink when they cook.

2 eggs, beaten
1/4 c. water
1/3 c. quick-cooking oats, uncooked
1.35-oz. pkg. onion soup mix
1 lb. lean ground chicken or turkey

19-oz. can lentils, drained and rinsed
4 buns or pita breads, split
Garnish: favorite burger toppings

Lightly beat eggs and water in a large bowl. Stir in oats and soup mix; let stand for 5 minutes. Add chicken or turkey and lentils. Mix well with your hands; shape into 4 patties. Cook on a countertop grill set on high for 5 to 6 minutes. Serve on buns or in split pita breads, garnished as desired. Makes 4 sandwiches.

Mix up a quick tomato salad to serve alongside sandwiches.
Cut juicy ripe tomatoes into cubes and toss with sliced
red onion, chopped fresh basil and your favorite
Italian salad dressing to taste.

Herb's 4-Day Grilled Teriyaki Chicken

Ann Brown
Niles, MI

I love the flavor of teriyaki sauce, but don't need all of the sugar and sodium, so I found a way to get the taste without the added sugar and sodium.

3 boneless, skinless chicken
   breasts, pounded thin
16-oz. can crushed pineapple
   in juice

3/4 c. low-sodium teriyaki sauce
6 T. brown sugar substitute,
   packed
cooked jasmine rice

Place chicken in a large plastic zipping bag; set aside. Combine pineapple with juice, teriyaki sauce and sugar substitute in a bowl; mix well and pour over chicken. Seal bag and refrigerate for 3 days, to allow chicken to absorb the flavors. On the fourth day, remove chicken from bag; set aside. Pour marinade into a saucepan; simmer over medium heat until heated through and set aside. Grill chicken on a countertop grill set on high for 5 to 6 minutes, until no longer pink and juices run clear. To serve, top chicken with some of the warm pineapple mixture; serve with rice. Makes 4 servings.

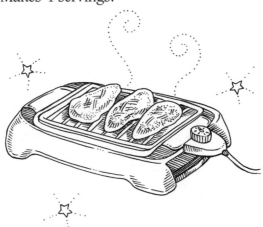

Whenever you grill chicken breasts for dinner, toss a couple of extra pieces on the grill. Sliced and refrigerated, they can be served another day in sandwich wraps or used to top a hearty salad for an easy meal with fresh-grilled flavor.

Jalapeño Buffalo Chicken

Samantha Ireland
Winterset, IA

Grill up a tasty lunch or dinner in just a few minutes!
Serve with Mexican sweet corn and warm tortillas.

1/4 c. onion, thinly sliced
1/4 c. canned jalapeño slices,
   quartered
2 to 3 t. butter
hot buffalo wing sauce to taste

1/8 t. pepper
1/2 t. dried parsley
1 boneless, skinless chicken
   breast

In a skillet over medium heat, sauté onion and jalapeño in butter.
Combine onion mixture, sauce, seasonings and chicken in a bowl;
stir. Transfer chicken to a countertop grill set on high; top with sauce
mixture. Grill chicken for 5 to 6 minutes, until no longer pink and juices
run clear. Drizzle with a little more sauce. Makes one serving.

"A Gal's Gotta Eat" Grilled Wrap

Julie Dossantos
Fort Pierce, FL

I often run home for lunch during the work week. I had all of
these ingredients left over from other meals, so I decided
to grill up a wrap...it was delicious!

1 whole-wheat tortilla wrap
1 slice baby Swiss cheese
1/4 c. sun-dried tomatoes

1/2 avocado, pitted, peeled
   and sliced
1/2 c. baby spinach

Place cheese slice in the center of tortilla wrap; top with remaining
ingredients in order listed. Roll up tortilla as tightly as possible. Cook on
a countertop or panini grill set on high for about 3 to 4 minutes. Cut
wrap in half to serve. Makes one wrap.

Handy Kitchen Helpers
• COUNTERTOP GRILL •

Chicken Pesto Panini

Trisha Cooper
Spanish Fork, UT

A really delicious sandwich...you may already have the ingredients for it! I like the mayonnaise & pesto sauce so much that sometimes I'll double it.

1 T. mayonnaise
1 t. basil pesto sauce
2 slices focaccia or country-style white bread
2 slices mozzarella cheese

1 to 2 slices cooked chicken breast
thinly sliced onion and green pepper, as desired

Combine mayonnaise and pesto in a cup; spread on one side of both bread slices. On one slice bread, layer cheese, chicken and vegetables; top with remaining bread. Place sandwich on a countertop or panini grill; cook on high setting until golden and cheese is melted, 3 to 5 minutes. Makes one sandwich.

Whip up some homemade basil pesto for fresh-from-the-garden taste. Just blend 2 cups fresh basil, 3 tablespoons pine nuts, 2 cloves garlic, 1/2 cup grated Parmesan cheese and 1/2 cup olive oil in a food processor...delicious!

Whipping Cream Waffles & Cranberry Butter

Kathy Grashoff
Fort Wayne, IN

I just love waffles on a snowy morning with nowhere to rush off to!

8-oz. container whipping cream
2 eggs, separated
1 T. butter, melted and slightly
   cooled

2/3 c. all-purpose flour
1/3 c. sugar
1 t. baking powder
1/8 t. salt

In a deep bowl, beat cream with an electric mixer on medium speed until soft peaks form. In a separate bowl, beat egg yolks with a fork until thick and light-colored; fold in whipped cream and butter. Combine remaining ingredients in a small bowl; fold into whipped cream mixture. Beat egg whites on high speed until stiff peaks form; fold into batter. Batter will be thick. For each waffle, spoon half of batter onto a preheated, oiled waffle iron, spreading to edges. Bake according to manufacturer's directions, until crisp and lightly golden. Serve with Cranberry Butter. Makes 2 servings.

Cranberry Butter:

1/2 c. butter, softened
1/4 c. powdered sugar

2 T. whole-berry cranberry sauce

Combine butter and powdered sugar; beat with an electric mixer on medium speed until blended. Stir in cranberry sauce; chill.

Watch for old-fashioned cream pitchers at tag sales...
set out a variety of sweet toppings like flavored syrups
and honey for fluffy pancakes and waffles.

Herb Waffles

Melanie Lowe
Dover, DE

Serve these flavorful waffles alongside scrambled eggs,
or topped with a scoop of your favorite creamed chicken.

2 c. all-purpose flour
2 T. sugar
4 t. baking powder
1 t. salt
2 T. fresh chives, snipped
1 T. fresh thyme, snipped

1 T. fresh flat-leaf parsley,
  snipped
1 T. fresh sage, snipped
1-1/2 c. milk
1/2 c. plus 2 T. butter
2 eggs, beaten

In a large bowl, mix together flour, sugar, baking powder and salt; stir in herbs. In a saucepan over low heat, warm milk and butter together until butter is melted. Cool slightly; whisk in eggs, then flour mixture. Pour 3/4 cup batter per waffle onto a preheated, buttered waffle iron. Bake according to manufacturer's directions, until crisp and golden. Makes 4 servings.

There's no limit to tasty waffle toppings! Try topping a sweet waffle with thinly sliced apples and a drizzle of caramel topping. A savory waffle is a perfect platform for Eggs Benedict, topped with Canadian bacon, poached eggs and hollandaise sauce. The sky's the limit!

Stuff-Yourself Waffles

Jill Ball
Highland, UT

Easy, yummy and fun! My older kids love to make these waffle sandwiches all by themselves as an after-school snack.

1 T. olive oil
4 eggs, lightly beaten
salt and pepper to taste
16-oz. tube refrigerated
    buttermilk biscuits

8 slices Cheddar cheese
8 slices thinly sliced ham

Heat oil in a skillet over medium high heat. Add eggs and scramble until lightly set; season with salt and pepper. Set aside. Separate biscuits, splitting each in half to create 16 pieces. Preheat a waffle iron to medium-high; spray with non-stick vegetable spray. Working in batches, add biscuit halves to waffle iron. Top each with cheese, ham, eggs and remaining biscuit half. Close gently; cook until crisp and golden, about 3 to 4 minutes. Serve immediately. Makes 8 servings.

Maple-Bacon Hashbrown Waffles

Dale-Harriet Rogovich
Madison, WI

No need to get out the skillet for crispy breakfast hashbrowns!

30-oz. pkg. frozen shredded
    hashbrowns, thawed
1/4 c. onion, finely chopped

2 T. real bacon bits
pure maple syrup to taste
salt and pepper to taste

Drain hashbrowns; squeeze dry with paper towels. Mix with remaining ingredients in a large bowl. Preheat a waffle iron to medium-high; spray with non-stick vegetable spray. For each waffle, spread one cup of hashbrown mixture on waffle iron. Cook for 7 to 8 minutes, until crisp and golden. Serves 4.

Special Waffle Sandwiches *Constance Bockstoce*
Dallas, GA

One day, I was out of bread for sandwiches. I thought, "Why not use waffles instead?" It's become a family favorite! Some combos we like are egg & sausage sandwiches for breakfast, rotisserie chicken salad sandwiches for lunch and Sloppy Joe sandwiches (swap out the cheese to sharp Cheddar) for a hearty dinner sandwich.

2 c. biscuit baking mix
1-1/2 c. water
2 T. olive oil
8-oz. pkg. finely shredded
   Swiss cheese

8 to 12 slices deli baked ham
2 to 3 ripe tomatoes, sliced
mayonnaise or other sandwich
   spread to taste

In a bowl, combine baking mix, water, oil and cheese; mix well. Add 3/4 cup batter per waffle to a greased waffle iron. Bake according to manufacturer's directions. Divide waffles into quarters. Top half of the waffle quarters with ham, tomato and mayonnaise; top with remaining quarters. Makes 4 to 6 servings.

French Toast Ham Sandwiches *Rita Morgan*
Pueblo, CO

Jazz up some ham sandwiches in a jiffy on a waffle iron.

12 slices bread
1/2 lb. thinly sliced deli baked
   ham
3 eggs, beaten

1/2 c. milk
1 t. sugar
1/4 t. salt
1/4 c. butter, softened

Assemble 6 sandwiches using bread and ham; set aside. Whisk together eggs, milk, sugar and salt in a shallow bowl. Dip each sandwich into egg mixture. Cook one sandwich at a time on a preheated, buttered waffle iron, about 5 minutes per side, until crisp and golden. Makes 6 sandwiches.

For lighter-than-air waffles, use club soda instead of milk or water in the batter.

Corn Waffle Tostadas

*Angela Murphy
Tempe, AZ*

My whole family loves this new way to enjoy Mexican tostadas.

1 lb. lean ground beef
3/4 c. water
1-oz. pkg. taco seasoning mix
8-1/2 oz. pkg. corn muffin mix
1/2 c. milk
1 egg, beaten

2 T. shortening, melted
Garnish: shredded lettuce,
  shredded Cheddar cheese,
  diced tomatoes, sliced green
  onions, sour cream

Brown beef in a skillet over medium heat. Drain; stir in water and taco seasoning. Meanwhile, beat together corn muffin mix, milk, egg and shortening. Add 3/4 cup batter per waffle to a preheated, greased waffle iron. Bake according to manufacturer's directions. Top waffles with beef mixture; garnish as desired. Serves 6.

Spicy-Sweet Corn Waffles

*Diana Chaney
Olathe, KS*

*Something different for breakfast or brunch! Or cut into
"fingers" for dipping into chili.*

3 canned chipotle peppers
  in adobo sauce
3/4 c. milk
2 c. biscuit baking mix

14-3/4 oz. can cream-style corn
2 T. oil
1 egg, beaten
Optional: maple syrup

Combine peppers and milk in a blender. Process until smooth; set aside. Mix remaining ingredients except syrup in a large bowl; add pepper mixture. Stir until combined. For each waffle, add 3/4 cup batter to a preheated, greased waffle iron. Bake according to manufacturer's directions, until crisp and golden. Serve with maple syrup, if desired. Makes 6 servings.

Freeze extra waffles, then reheat in a toaster for a fast weekday meal.

Chicken & Waffles

Vickie
Gooseberry Patch

Such an unusual combination...but you're going to love every bite! Serve with your favorite waffles, or try one of the waffle recipes in this chapter.

2 lbs. chicken thighs and
    drumsticks
2 c. buttermilk
1/2 c. all-purpose flour
1/2 c. cornstarch
1/2 t. cayenne pepper

1/2 t. garlic powder
1/2 t. onion powder
1 t. Italian seasoning
1 c. shortening
4 waffles
Garnish: maple syrup or honey

Place chicken in a large plastic zipping bag; add buttermilk. Seal bag and refrigerate for at least 4 hours. Remove chicken from bag, discarding buttermilk. Pat chicken dry with paper towels; set aside. In a shallow bowl, combine flour, cornstarch and seasonings; mix well. Dredge chicken in flour mixture; shake off any excess. Heat shortening in a large heavy skillet, to about 365 degrees. Cook chicken, 4 to 5 pieces at a time, for 4 to 7 minutes per side, until crisp and juices run clear when pierced. Serve chicken on waffles; drizzle with maple syrup or honey. Serves 4.

For easy release, most waffle irons need to be greased. A silicone basting brush is perfect for brushing oil or softened butter over every nook and cranny...afterwards, just toss the brush in the dishwasher!

Chocolate Waffle Sundaes
Phyl Broich-Wessling
Garner, IA

Ice cream on a crisp chocolate waffle...what could be better for dessert, or even for a breakfast treat on a special day?

1-1/4 c. chocolate milk
1 egg, beaten
2 T. shortening, melted
1 c. buttermilk biscuit
    baking mix

1/2 gal. vanilla ice cream
Garnish: chopped, toasted
    pecans, walnuts or hazelnuts,
    sliced bananas and
    strawberries

Combine milk, egg and shortening in a large bowl. Add baking mix; whisk until smooth. Add 3/4 cup batter per waffle to a preheated, greased waffle iron. Bake according to manufacturer's directions. To serve, top each waffle with 2 scoops of ice cream; garnish as desired. Serves 6.

Treat yourself! Stir up some 5-minute chocolate sauce to drizzle over waffle sundaes or even over breakfast waffles! In a small saucepan, combine 1/3 cup sweet or dark chocolate and 2/3 cup cream. Cook and stir over low heat until melted and smooth. Remove from heat and let stand for several minutes, until thickened. Enjoy!

Waffle Cookies

Bonnie Baker
Mansfield, OH

This recipe was given to my mother-in-law in the 1970s by a dear friend, and we have been making these cookies ever since. They are always the first cookies we make every Christmas. It's a fun family project, with jobs for everyone...from mixing them up, to watching the waffle iron and dusting with the powdered sugar!

6 c. all-purpose flour
2 c. brown sugar, packed
2 c. sugar
8 eggs, beaten

1 lb. margarine, melted and
    slightly cooled
1 T. vanilla
Garnish: powdered sugar

Mix flour and sugars in a very large bowl; make a well in the center. Add eggs, melted margarine and vanilla to the well; beat until well mixed. Drop batter by egg-size portions into the center of each section of a greased, preheated waffle iron. Bake on medium-high for about 2 minutes. Sprinkle cookies with powdered sugar while still warm. Store in an airtight container. Makes about 6 dozen.

Dip cooled cookies halfway into melted white chocolate for a yummy treat. Set on wax paper to cool...add some candy sprinkles just for fun!

Cheesy Macaroni Beef

Sherry Prescott
Winchester, IN

An easy supper dish! I first tried this recipe in a high school cooking class, 40 years ago. It's been a favorite since then because it's so easy to put together at the last minute, with items most everyone has on hand.

1/4 c. butter, sliced
2 c. elbow macaroni, uncooked
4 c. tomato juice
1 lb. lean ground beef
1 onion, chopped

1 t. salt
1/2 t. pepper
4 to 6 slices pasteurized process
   cheese

Melt butter in an electric skillet. Add uncooked macaroni; stir until coated. Add tomato juice and bring to a rapid boil. Add uncooked beef in small chunks, onion, salt and pepper. Cover and cook at 250 degrees for 20 minutes, or until beef is cooked and macaroni is tender. Uncover and stir. Arrange cheese slices on top; cover and cook just until cheese is melted. Makes 4 servings.

Easy Skillet Pizza

Kerry Mayer
Dunham Springs, LA

My daughter Kim and I like to whip up this yummy pizza together whenever it's just the two of us for dinner.

1-1/2 c. buttermilk baking mix
3/4 c. milk
15-oz. can pizza sauce
1/2 lb. pepperoni slices
2 t. Italian seasoning

1 c. sliced mushrooms
Optional: other favorite pizza
   toppings
1 c. shredded pizza-blend cheese

Combine baking mix and milk in a bowl; stir until a soft dough forms. Grease the bottom and sides of a cold electric skillet; press dough into bottom and sides of skillet. Spread sauce over crust; sprinkle with seasoning. Arrange pepperoni slices, mushrooms and other toppings on crust as desired; sprinkle with cheese. Set skillet temperature to 325 degrees. Cover and bake for 20 minutes, or until cheese is melted and crust is golden. Cut into wedges. Makes 6 servings.

Handy Kitchen Helpers
• ELECTRIC SKILLET •

Aunt Pauline's Fried Apple Pies

Janice Tarter
Morrow, OH

My Aunt Pauline is a fabulous country cook! She never follows a recipe, never measures, but turns out the best southern food around. Her fried apple pies have always been one of her most-requested dishes. I took her "recipe" calling for "a lot of this, a bit of that," and came up with one we could all follow. These little hand pies are good for breakfast, brunch, or dessert...they keep well too.

2 T. butter	12-oz. can refrigerated biscuits
1/4 c. sugar	1/2 c. shortening
2 t. cinnamon	Optional: 1 c. powdered sugar
2 t. allspice	and 2 to 4 tablespoons water,
1 t. ground cloves	or cinnamon-sugar to taste
8 cooking apples, peeled, cored and thinly sliced	

Melt butter in a saucepan over medium heat. Stir in sugar, spices and apple slices. Sauté apples until tender; remove from heat and cool. Meanwhile, separate biscuits; flatten each biscuit into a circle. Spoon some of apple filling into each biscuit. Fold biscuits in half to form pies; use the tines of a fork to crimp edges. Turn an electric skillet to 350 degrees; melt shortening in skillet. Add 5 pies and cook until golden, about 5 minutes; turn and cook the other side. Remove pies to a plate; repeat with remaining pies. If desired, combine powdered sugar and enough water to make a thin glaze; drizzle over pies. Instead of glaze, pies may be sprinkled with cinnamon-sugar. Makes 10 pies.

Whip up a tasty apple cider glaze. Mix up 1-1/4 cups powdered sugar and 3/4 teaspoon apple pie spice. Stir in 2 tablespoons apple cider until a drizzling consistency is reached.

Chilled Gazpacho Soup

Suzanne Alexander
South Point, OH

I love growing tomatoes and can't wait until the first ones are ripe to make this recipe. I grow the cucumbers and parsley that go into this recipe. It's fresh and fabulous for summertime.

2 to 3 ripe tomatoes, coarsely chopped
1/3 c. cucumber, peeled and coarsely chopped
1/3 c. celery, chopped
3 T. sweet onion, chopped
1 c. cocktail vegetable juice or tomato juice

2 T. fresh parsley, chopped
2 T. red wine vinegar or cider vinegar
2 T. olive oil
2 t. lime juice
1/2 t. paprika
1/2 t. salt
1/8 t. pepper

Combine all ingredients in a blender. Cover and process for about 5 seconds, until well mixed but not puréed. Transfer soup to a large bowl; cover and refrigerate for at least an hour before serving. Ladle into small bowls to serve. Serves 4 to 6.

Make a double batch of Chilled Gazpacho Soup and ladle into jelly jars. Tuck a jar into a basket along with a couple of fresh corn muffins, as a lunchtime surprise for a friend. Sure to be welcome on a warm day!

Cool Cucumber-Avocado Soup

Sharon Jones
Oklahoma City, OK

Chilled soup is great to eat in the summer when it's too hot to cook. Served with a fresh tossed salad, this is delicious.

1 lb. cucumbers, peeled and
    coarsely chopped
2 avocados, halved, peeled
    and cubed
1/4 c. lime juice

3/4 c. water
1 t. salt
1/2 t. pepper
Optional: chopped tomato,
    snipped fresh cilantro

Combine all ingredients except optional garnish in a blender. Cover and process until smooth. Season with more salt and pepper, if desired. Transfer soup to a large bowl; cover and refrigerate for at least an hour before serving. Garnish each serving with tomato and cilantro, if desired. Serves 4.

For a speedy Greek salad that can be made any time of year, combine quartered roma tomatoes with sliced black olives, crumbled feta cheese and chopped red onion. Drizzle with Italian salad dressing and toss to mix.

Andrea's Pineapple Salsa

Andrea Heyart
Savannah, TX

This is what I crave when I crave salsa! This recipe can be adjusted to how spicy (more jalapeños and cilantro) or sweet (more pineapple) you like your salsa.

4 to 5 ripe tomatoes, coarsely chopped
1/2 c. yellow onion, coarsely chopped
1 clove garlic, coarsely chopped
1 to 2 jalapeño peppers, chopped and seeded

1 T. fresh cilantro, chopped
juice of 1 lime
1 t. cider vinegar
1/2 c. fresh or canned pineapple chunks
salt to taste

Combine all ingredients in a food processor or blender. Cover; pulse blender 3 to 4 times to desired consistency. Transfer salsa to a bowl; cover and refrigerate 2 hours for best flavor. Serves 6 to 10.

Delicious Dipping Sauce

MaryBeth Summers
Medford, OR

My grandson's favorite condiment! Great with fried shrimp, fried clams, chicken fingers, chicken wings or over fried rice.

10-3/4 oz. can tomato soup
1 T. dry mustard
1 c. oil
1/2 c. sugar

1/2 c. white vinegar
Worcestershire sauce to taste
Optional: prepared horseradish to taste

Combine all ingredients in a blender; cover and process until smooth. Transfer to a bowl; cover and refrigerate until chilled. Serves 6.

May the roof above us never fall in, and may we friends gathered here never fall out.
– Irish Blessing

Handy Kitchen Helpers
• BLENDER •

Easy Peach Salsa

Kristin Freeman
Dundas, MN

A friend of mine shared this quick & easy recipe with me.
Enjoy it with white corn tortilla chips.

2 14-1/2 oz. cans Mexican-
   seasoned stewed tomatoes
1 jalapeño pepper, seeded

15-oz. can can sliced peaches in
   light syrup
Optional: salt to taste

Add tomatoes with juice and jalapeño pepper to a blender; cover and
process to desired texture. Transfer to a bowl; set aside. Add peaches
with syrup to blender and process to desired texture; add to tomato
mixture and stir together. Season with salt, if desired. Serves 8 to 10.

Blender Hummus

Kathy Grashoff
Fort Wayne, IN

This is quick for drop-ins! Take it out on your deck and enjoy.

15-oz. can garbanzo beans,
   drained
juice of 4 lemons
3 cloves garlic, pressed

1 t. Asian sesame oil
salt to taste
pita chips, cut-up vegetables

In a blender, combine all ingredients except chips and vegetables.
Cover and process until smooth. If too thick, add a little water, one to
2 teaspoons at a time, until desired consistency. Transfer to a bowl;
cover and refrigerate. Serve pita chips and vegetables. Makes about
1-1/2 cups.

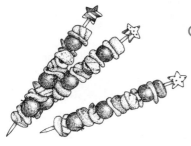

Guests will love these dippers! Thread
carrot and celery slices, cauliflower
and broccoli flowerets and olives
onto small wooden skewers in
different combinations...arrange
around a selection of yummy dips.

Orange Julius

Julie Snow
Park Rapids, MN

I used to love the Orange Julius stand in the mall when I was a kid. With a little help from my mom, we were able to come up with this recipe...I think it's even better!

1/2 c. frozen orange juice
   concentrate
1/2 c. milk

2-1/2 T. sugar
1 t. vanilla extract
ice cubes

Combine all ingredients except ice cubes in a blender. Cover and process for 30 seconds. Add ice cubes, one at a time; process until thickened. Pour into a tall glass; serve immediately. Serves one.

Booster Sunrise Smoothie

Shirl Parsons
Cape Carteret, NC

Give yourself a great boost in the morning with this refreshing fruit smoothie.

1 c. orange juice
1 c. low-fat vanilla frozen yogurt
1 banana, cut into chunks

1/2 c. egg substitute or
   pasteurized egg

Combine all ingredients in a blender. Cover and process until smooth; pour into 2 glasses. Makes 2 servings.

Dress up a tall glass of your favorite blender drink.
Simply make a small cut in an orange slice and a
whole strawberry and tuck over the edge of the glass.

Handy Kitchen Helpers
• BLENDER •

Berry-Cheesecake Smoothie
Lisa McClelland
Columbus, OH

The perfect treat! Mom would let us help her make this for a snack and to help us learn our way around the kitchen.

1-1/2 c. frozen strawberry yogurt
3/4 c. blueberry-pomegranate
   cocktail juice
1/4 c. low-fat sour cream

3 T. cream cheese
2 to 3 c. frozen mixed berries
Garnish: graham crackers

Put everything except frozen berries and garnish in a blender and blend. Add the frozen berries and blend til smooth. Pour into 2 large glasses; serve with graham crackers for dipping. Serves 2.

Chocolate-Cherry Shake
Marla Kinnersley
Surprise, AZ

This has been the most-requested smoothie at our home. It tastes like ice cream and is so quick and simple to make.

2 c. frozen cherries
1 c. unsweetened almond milk

1 c. plain Greek yogurt
2 T. baking cocoa

Blend well in a blender. For a thinner consistency, add more almond milk. Divide between 2 tall glasses. Serves 2.

Clean your blender in a jiffy! Fill halfway with hot water and add a drop of dish soap. Holding a towel on the lid, process for about 10 seconds. Pour out the soapy water and rinse with fresh water...done!

Frozen Hot Chocolate

Judy Palkovic
Freedom, PA

A delicious variation on the hot variety! Perfect for celebrating Christmas in July...cute served with a tall candy cane in each glass.

1 qt. vanilla ice cream	4 t. cinnamon
1 qt. cold milk	1 c. ice cubes
2 c. chocolate syrup, divided	1 c. marshmallow creme

In a bowl, break ice cream into chunks. In a blender, working in batches, combine ice cream, milk, 1-1/2 cups chocolate syrup, cinnamon and ice. Pulse until thick, creamy and no ice crystals remain. Pour mixture into 8 tall glasses. Top each with 2 tablespoons marshmallow creme and one tablespoon remaining chocolate syrup. Serves 8.

Need a cup or two of powdered sugar, yet all you have on hand is granulated sugar? No problem...use your blender! Pour sugar into the blender and process until fluffy and finely powdered. One-half cup regular sugar will blend up to about one cup powdered sugar.

Handy Kitchen Helpers
• BLENDER •

Strawberry-Pineapple Ice

Jennifer Niemi
Nova Scotia, Canada

*Looks lovely in wine glasses...can be stored frozen in
airtight container for up to 2 weeks.*

2 10-oz. pkgs. frozen
   strawberries, thawed

14-oz. can crushed pineapple
1 T. lemon juice

Purée undrained strawberries and pineapple in a blender. Strain through
a fine mesh strainer; press with back of spoon as necessary to extract all
the juice. Discard pulp. Stir in lemon juice. Pour into a chilled freezer-
safe glass or ceramic bowl. Cover with plastic wrap; freeze overnight. At
serving time, scrape with a fork into serving dishes. Serves 6.

Strawberry Blender Dessert

Leona Krivda
Belle Vernon, PA

This is a fun dessert, and something different.

6-oz. pkg. strawberry gelatin mix
12-oz. pkg. frozen strawberries,
   thawed
8-oz. pkg. cream cheese, cubed

2 c. boiling water
Garnish: whipped topping,
   whole strawberries

Combine all ingredients in a blender. Process on high for one minute.
Pour into 6 serving dishes; cover and chill. Garnish portions with
whipped topping and a strawberry. Serves 6.

Heat limes or lemons in the microwave for 30 seconds
before squeezing...you'll get twice the juice!

Minnesota Battered Fish & Chips

Rogene Rogers
Kalispell, MT

I used to live in Minnesota, where there are always plenty of lakes to catch fresh fish! We love beer-battered fish, and this recipe is a very easy one. The chips or fries are fried twice to get that good restaurant-style crispness.

1-1/4 c. all-purpose flour
12-oz. can regular or
  non-alcoholic beer
4 russet potatoes, peeled

oil for deep-frying
4 firm white fish fillets
1/4 c. cornstarch
Garnish: lemon wedges

Add flour to a bowl; gradually whisk in beer to make a smooth batter. Set aside. Cut potatoes into fries, about 3/4 inch thick; soak for 10 minutes in cold water. Drain and pat dry. Fill a deep fryer 2/3 full with oil; heat until a cube of bread browns in 30 seconds. Add the fries in batches and cook for 4 to 5 minutes, until pale golden. Remove with tongs or a slotted spoon; drain on paper towels and set aside. Pat fish fillets dry with paper towels. Lightly dust with cornstarch; dip into batter. Deep-fry fish fillets in batches for 5 to 7 minutes, until golden and cooked through. Drain on paper towels; keep warm. Just before serving, reheat oil until a cube of bread browns in 15 seconds. Re-cook fries in batches until crisp and golden; drain. Serve with lemon wedges. Serves 4.

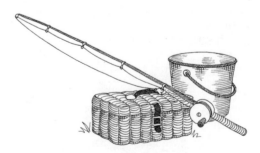

The best oil for deep frying? Look for the one labeled simply "vegetable oil." It has a neutral taste and a high smoke point, which is important. Other good choices are peanut, safflower and canola oil.

Deep-Fried Steak Nuggets

Jason Nicholson
Gooseberry Patch

At our football parties, the guys can't get enough of these!
There are a couple of day-before steps, but they're
worth it. At party time, just deep-fry and serve.

1-1/2 lbs. boneless beef top
   sirloin, sliced 1/4-inch thick
1 egg, beaten
2 c. buttermilk
3 c. all-purpose flour, divided
2 T. Montreal steak seasoning

2 t. garlic powder
salt and pepper to taste
3 c. canola oil
Garnish: ranch salad dressing or
   favorite steak sauce

Cut steak strips into 2-1/2 inch pieces; set aside. In a large bowl, beat together egg, buttermilk, 1/2 cup flour and steak seasoning until smooth. Add steak; toss until well coated. Cover bowl with plastic wrap; refrigerate at least 2 hours. In a shallow bowl, combine remaining flour and seasonings. Remove steak strips from batter; allow excess to drip off. Coat with seasoned flour; arrange on a baking sheet. Cover and freeze until firm, one hour to overnight. Add oil to a deep fryer; heat to 370 degrees. Working in batches, add several frozen steak strips; cook until golden, about 5 minutes. (Do not allow steak to thaw before being fried.) Drain on paper towels. Serve with desired garnish. Serves 4.

It is amazing how much the little niceties of life
have to do with making a dinner pleasant.
– Book of Etiquette by Lillian Eichler, 1921

Tina's Famous Corn Dogs

Tina Goodpasture
Meadowview, VA

Everyone down south loves corn dogs! They are even better homemade...I think mine are the best!

12 wooden skewers	1 egg
12 hot dogs	1 T. sugar
3/4 c. all-purpose flour	oil for deep frying
1/4 c. cornmeal	Garnish: mustard
1/2 c. milk	

Insert skewers into hot dogs; set aside. In a deep bowl, combine remaining ingredients except garnish; mix well. Heat several inches of oil in a deep fryer. Dip hot dogs into batter. Add hot dogs to fryer, one at a time; cook until golden. Drain on paper towels. Serve with mustard for dipping. Serves 12.

Jackie's Chicken Nuggets

Jackie Hatfield
Shepherdsville, KY

My son asks for these all the time. Serve with your favorite dipping sauce...yummy!

1 c. biscuit baking mix	oil for deep frying
3/4 c. water	Optional: favorite dipping
4 to 5 boneless, skinless chicken	sauces
breasts, cut into cubes	

Combine baking mix and water, making batter just a little thicker than for pancakes. Heat several inches of oil in a deep fryer. Dip chicken nuggets into batter. Add nuggets to hot oil, a few at a time; cook until golden and juices run clear when pierced. Drain on paper towels. Serve with dipping sauces, if desired. Serves 5 to 7.

Great for kids' parties... serve finger foods on a plastic flying disc for each child. What fun!

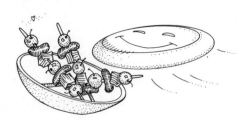

Firecracker Shrimp

Ashley Jones
Gates, NC

A recipe I learned and tweaked to make at home,
from one of my favorite places to eat!

1 c. mayonnaise
1/4 c. sriracha hot sauce
1/2 c. honey
3 T. dried parsley
1/8 t. salt

1 lb. uncooked jumbo shrimp,
   peeled and cleaned
1 c. all-purpose flour
oil for deep frying
Garnish: additional dried parsley

In a bowl, combine mayonnaise, honey, hot sauce and seasonings. Mix well and set aside. Add flour to a shallow bowl; coat shrimp in flour. Heat several inches of oil in a deep fryer. Add shrimp to hot oil, a few at a time; cook for about 5 minutes. Drain shrimp on paper towels. When all the shrimp is fried, transfer shrimp to a bowl. Drizzle with mayonnaise mixture; toss to coat evenly. Sprinkle with more parsley and serve. Serves 3 to 4.

Done at the right temperature, deep-fried foods aren't greasy. The ideal temperature range is 350 to 375 degrees. If you don't have a deep-frying thermometer, drop a cube of bread into the hot oil. If it turns golden in 60 seconds, the oil is ready.

Oriental Chicken Salad

Marianne Hilgenberg
Orlando, FL

I've been making this unusual chicken salad for years. It's been handed down so many times and has been shared across the world, literally...I have friends in Germany, England & Scotland!

1 egg
1/2 c. milk
1/2 c. all-purpose flour
1/2 c. corn flake cereal, crushed
1 t. salt
1/4 t. pepper
1 boneless, skinless chicken
   breast, cut into 4 to
   5 long strips

2 to 4 c. oil for deep frying
3 c. romaine lettuce, chopped
1 c. red cabbage, shredded
1 c. napa cabbage, shredded
1/2 carrot, peeled and shredded
1 green onion, chopped
1 T. sliced almonds
1/3 c. chow mein noodles

Make Oriental Dressing ahead of time; chill. In a shallow bowl, whisk together egg and milk; set aside. In another shallow bowl, combine flour, corn flake crumbs, salt and pepper. Dip each chicken strip first into egg mixture, then into flour mixture, coating completely. Heat oil in a deep fryer to about 350 degrees. Cook chicken strips for 5 minutes, or until coating has darkened to brown. Drain on paper towels; cut chicken into bite-size chunks and set aside. In a salad bowl, combine lettuce, cabbages and carrot; sprinkle with onion, almonds and noodles. Heap chicken onto center of salad; serve with Oriental Dressing on the side. Makes 2 to 4 servings.

Oriental Dressing:

1/4 c. mayonnaise
3 T. honey
1-1/2 T. rice wine vinegar

1 t. Dijon mustard
1/8 t. sesame oil

In a small bowl, beat all ingredients with an electric mixer on low speed until blended; cover and chill.

Handy Kitchen Helpers
• DEEP FRYER •

Football Wings

Samantha Gonzales
Morrison, IL

I make these tasty wings for my family to enjoy while we're watching football. Be sure to have plenty of cool beverages on hand!

3 c. all-purpose flour
3 t. onion powder
2 t. chili powder
1 t. pepper
3 t. garlic powder, divided

1 t. paprika, divided
oil for frying
5 lbs. chicken wings, separated
1/2 c. butter
2 c. hot pepper sauce

In a large container with a lid, combine flour, onion powder, chili powder, pepper, 2 teaspoons garlic powder and 1/2 teaspoon paprika. Add wings; cover and toss until well coated. Place wings in deep fryer basket; set aside. Heat several inches of oil in a deep fryer to 375 degrees. Add wings in basket; cook for 20 to 25 minutes, until golden and juices run clear. Meanwhile, melt butter in a saucepan over low heat. Add hot sauce and remaining garlic powder and paprika. Bring just to a boil; remove from heat. When wings are done, add to sauce mixture. Toss well and serve hot. Makes about 5 dozen.

For the crispest chicken wings, corn dogs, French fries and other fried foods, drain them on a wire rack that's been set over a paper towel-lined baking sheet.

Deep-Fried Corn on the Cob
Dana Lungerich
Frisco, TX

This is a recipe from my (adopted) grandmother Barbara Robertson. She was a neighbor my entire life, and loved me like I was her own grandchild. When she passed away, I inherited her recipe box.

1-1/2 c. yellow cornmeal
1 c. grated Parmesan cheese
2/3 c. all-purpose flour
2 T. garlic salt
1-1/2 c. milk
2 eggs, beaten
1/4 c. oil

2 c. corn flake cereal, crushed
oil for deep frying
6 ears sweet corn, husked and
broken in half
salt and pepper to taste
Optional: ranch salad dressing

In a large bowl, combine cornmeal, cheese, flour, garlic salt, milk, eggs and 1/4 cup oil. Mix well to a pancake batter consistency; set aside. Place crushed cereal in a shallow dish. In a deep fryer, heat several inches oil to 375 degrees. Dip each piece of corn into batter and roll in crumbs; cook for 2 to 3 minutes, until golden. Drain on paper towels; sprinkle with salt and pepper. Serve with salad dressing, if desired. Serves 6.

Watch yard sales for a vintage salad dressing server...
it's just as handy for serving up a variety of creamy
dips and sauces for party foods.

Deep-Fried Pimento Cheese & Celery Bites

Debra Elliott
Trussville, AL

*Growing up in the south, I ate a lot of pimento cheese on celery.
I took a southern classic and turned it into deep-fried goodness.*

12-oz. container pimento cheese
1 stalk celery, finely chopped
1 egg, beaten
1/2 c. Italian-seasoned dry
   bread crumbs

1 t. seasoned salt
1/2 t. paprika
1/4 c. all-purpose flour
2 to 3 c. oil for deep frying
Garnish: ranch salad dressing

In a bowl, combine cheese, celery, egg, bread crumbs and seasoning; mix well and set aside. Place flour in a shallow dish. Lightly spray an ice cream scoop with non-stick vegetable spray. Scoop cheese mixture into small balls; roll balls in flour to coat lightly. Add oil to a deep fryer, filling about 3/4 full; heat to 375 degrees. Working in batches, add cheese balls and cook until golden. Remove to paper towels to drain. Serve with salad dressing. Serves 12 to 16.

Guests will welcome fresh veggie dippers like baby carrots, celery stalks and broccoli flowerets. Serve with a creamy dill dip made of one cup sour cream or plain Greek yogurt, 1/2 cup mayonnaise, 2 teaspoons dill weed and 2 teaspoons lemon juice. Chill overnight before serving.

Best-Ever Fritter Batter

Annette Ingram
Grand Rapids, MI

This versatile batter is great for deep-frying mushrooms, dill pickles,
chunks of chicken or pork...whatever sounds good to you!

4 c. vegetables, cubed, or
   1 lb. meat or fish, cubed
3/4 c. cornstarch
1/4 c. all-purpose flour
1 t. baking powder
1/2 t. salt

1/4 t. pepper
1/2 c. club soda or water, plus up
   to 1/2 c. more for thinning
1 egg, lightly beaten
oil for deep frying

Cut foods to be deep-fried into equal-size cubes or pieces; set aside. In a
bowl, combine cornstarch, flour, baking powder and seasonings. Add
soda or water and egg; whisk until smooth. In a deep fryer, heat several
inches oil to 375 degrees. Dip pieces; cook for several minutes, until
golden and cooked through. Drain on paper towels. Serves 4 to 6.

Myrtle Beach Corn Dodgers

Toni Currin
Dillon, SC

These hush puppy-like morsels are good with fried fish or
alongside a bowl of chili.

2 eggs, beaten
1-1/2 c. milk
2 c. cornmeal
1 c. all-purpose flour

1 T. baking powder
1/2 t. salt
oil for deep frying

In a bowl, whisk together eggs and milk; set aside. In a large bowl,
combine remaining ingredients; stir in egg mixture. In a deep fryer, heat
several inches oil to 350 degrees. Working in batches, drop batter into
oil by spoonfuls. Cook until golden on all sides. Makes 6 to 8 servings.

Cornmeal comes in both yellow and
white...the choice is yours!

Handy Kitchen Helpers
• DEEP FRYER •

Golden Onion Rings

Wendy Lee Paffenroth
Pine Island, NY

*Living in an area where lots of onions are grown, I have
so many recipes shared for all types of onions.
This is always a favorite for barbecues.*

4 large onions, thickly sliced and
   separated into rings
1-1/4 c. biscuit baking mix
1-1/2 t. brown sugar, packed
1/4 t. salt

1 c. regular or non-alcoholic beer
1 T. oil
4 egg whites
canola oil for deep frying

Place onion rings on paper towels to drain. Meanwhile, in a large bowl, mix together baking mix, brown sugar and salt. Pour in beer all at once; mixture will foam. Add one tablespoon oil; whisk together to make a batter. In a separate bowl, beat egg whites until frothy; fold into batter. In a deep fryer, heat several inches oil to 375 degrees. Dip onion rings into batter to coat. With a slotted spoon, add several onion rings to oil at a time; cook until golden. Drain on paper towels. Serves 6.

Stir up a super-simple yet scrumptious dipping sauce for onion rings! Combine 1/2 cup mayonnaise, 2 tablespoons catsup, one tablespoon horseradish sauce and 1/2 teaspoon paprika. Season with cayenne pepper, if you like it hot!

Southwest Egg Rolls

Jean Prindle
Montrose, IA

What an awesome surprise when you bite into one of these egg rolls!
Fun to prepare too. They can be made ahead of time and frozen,
then put into a deep fryer as needed.

1 lb. ground Italian pork sausage
1/2 c. onion, chopped
1/2 c. red and/or yellow pepper,
    chopped
15-oz. can refried beans
1-1/4 oz. pkg. taco seasoning mix

1/2 c. shredded Cheddar cheese
15 egg roll wrappers
shortening or peanut oil for
    deep frying
Garnish: sour cream, salsa

In a large skillet over medium heat, brown sausage with onion and pepper; drain well. Add beans, seasoning mix and cheese; stir until well blended and cheese is melted. Spoon 1/4 cup into the center of an egg roll wrapper. Brush edges of wrapper with a little water; fold one corner over filling. Fold opposite corners to center; roll up and seal remaining corner. Repeat with remaining ingredients. In a deep fryer, heat several inches shortening or oil to 375 degrees. Add egg rolls, a few at a time; cook until golden. Serve with sour cream and salsa for dipping. Makes 15 servings.

Real cloth napkins make mealtime just a little more special, and they're earth-friendly too...no paper napkins to throw away. Stitch fun charms to napkin rings, so everyone can identify their own napkin easily.

Deep-Fried Jalapeño Slices

Deanna Isabelle
Quinlan, TX

My husband and father love jalapeño peppers, so I decided to fry them. They were a big hit!

1 c. all-purpose flour
1 t. chili powder
1 t. garlic powder
1 t. salt
1 t. pepper

2 eggs, beaten
1 c. regular or non-alcoholic beer
2 c. oil for deep frying
2 c. jalapeño peppers, sliced and
    seeds removed

Mix together flour, seasonings, eggs and beer in a bowl; set aside. In a deep fryer, heat several inches oil to 365 degrees. Dip jalapeño slices into batter; add to oil, a few at a time. Cook until jalapeños are crisp, golden and float to the surface of oil. Drain on paper towels. Serves 4.

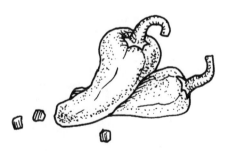

When slicing and chopping hot jalapeño peppers, plastic
gloves are a must to prevent skin irritation. Be sure not to
touch your face, lips or eyes while you're working!
Afterwards, just toss away the gloves.

Caramel-Drizzled Apple Fritters

Denise Evans
Moosic, PA

I love anything that ends in "fritters," and anything is good with caramel drizzled over it. This recipe is a little indulgent, but once in a while I think that's good for our souls. The guilt-free way to eat these is to promise yourself you will take a little walk when you're done eating them. There, you see...you just treated yourself to a walk around the block as well!

1 c. all-purpose flour	oil for deep frying
1-1/2 t. baking powder	5 to 6 tart apples, peeled, cored
2 T. sugar	and cut into wedges
1/2 t. salt	Garnish: caramel ice cream
1/2 c. milk	topping
1 egg, well beaten	

In a shallow bowl, mix together flour, baking powder, sugar and salt. Add milk and egg; mix well. In a deep fryer, heat several inches oil to 370 degrees. Dip each piece of apple into batter. Working in batches, add to hot oil; cook until golden. Drain on paper towels. Arrange apples on a serving plate and drizzle with caramel topping, or place topping in a small bowl in center of plate for dipping. Serves 6 to 8.

Cutting up apples ahead of time? Here's a little secret...cut slices won't brown as fast if you use an extra-sharp knife.

Handy Kitchen Helpers
• DEEP FRYER •

Funnel Cakes

Janice Schuler
Alburtis, PA

A favorite treat at so many county fairs!

2 eggs, beaten
2 c. milk, warmed
2-1/2 to 3 c. all-purpose flour
2 T. sugar
1 t. baking powder

1 t. baking soda
1 t. salt
oil for deep frying
Garnish: powdered sugar

In a large bowl, whisk together eggs and warm milk. In a separate bowl, mix together flour, sugar, baking power, baking soda and salt. Add to egg mixture and stir well. Add several inches oil in a deep fryer; heat to 400 degrees. Pour 1/2 cup batter through a funnel, holding your finger over end of funnel and swirling funnel to make circles in oil. Cook until golden. Using tongs, remove funnel cake to a plate; dust with powdered sugar. Repeat with remaining ingredients. Makes 6 servings.

Whip up some homemade cherry pie filling to drizzle over funnel cakes...yum! Just combine one pound pitted tart cherries, 3/4 cup sugar, 1/3 cup cornstarch and 2 tablespoons lemon juice in a saucepan over medium heat. Bring to a boil, then simmer until thickened and cool.

INDEX

INDEX

INDEX

Find Gooseberry Patch
wherever you are!

www.gooseberrypatch.com

Call us toll-free at 1·800·854·6673

carefree cooking•it's a snap ... *make it easy* ... *(only easier)•pipinghot* ... *came & get it!* ... *make it easier•*

U.S. to Metric Recipe Equivalents

Volume Measurements

1/4 teaspoon	1 mL
1/2 teaspoon	2 mL
1 teaspoon	5 mL
1 tablespoon = 3 teaspoons	15 mL
2 tablespoons = 1 fluid ounce	30 mL
1/4 cup	60 mL
1/3 cup	75 mL
1/2 cup = 4 fluid ounces	125 mL
1 cup = 8 fluid ounces	250 mL
2 cups = 1 pint =16 fluid ounces	500 mL
4 cups = 1 quart	1 L

Weights

1 ounce	30 g
4 ounces	120 g
8 ounces	225 g
16 ounces = 1 pound	450 g

Oven Temperatures

300° F	150° C
325° F	160° C
350° F	180° C
375° F	190° C
400° F	200° C
450° F	230° C

Baking Pan Sizes

Square

8x8x2 inches	2 L = 20x20x5 cm
9x9x2 inches	2.5 L = 23x23x5 cm

Rectangular

13x9x2 inches	3.5 L = 33x23x5 cm

Loaf

9x5x3 inches	2 L = 23x13x7 cm

Round

8x1-1/2 inches	1.2 L = 20x4 cm
9x1-1/2 inches	1.5 L = 23x4 cm